# Joint Kicks

## Destruction of the Opponent's Limbs

### Take away an Attacker's Ability to Strike and to Move, Even if he is Pain-resistant

By

**Marc De Bremaeker**

*Fons Sapientiae Publishing*

**Joint Kicks – Destruction of the Opponent's Limbs**. Published in 2018 by Fons Sapientiae Publishing, Cambridge, United Kingdom

ISBN for the printed version: 978-0-9957952-4-2

*Recommended reading, by the same author*:
"Isoplex - Musculation Program for an Aesthetic and Truly Athlectic Body" (2017)
"Krav Maga Kicks - Kicking for No-nonsense Self-preservation" (2017)
"Sacrifice Kicks - Flying, Hopping, Jumping and Suicide Kicks" (2016)
"Stealth Kicks - The Forgotten Art of Ghost Kicking" (2015)
"Ground Kicks-Advanced Martial Arts Kicks for Goundfighting" (2015)
"Stop Kicks-Jamming, Obstructing, Stopping, Impaling, Cutting and Preemptive Kicks" (2014)
"Low kicks-Advanced Martial Arts Kicks for Attacking the Lower Gates" (2013)
"Plyo-Flex-Plyometrics and Flexibility Training for Explosive Martial Arts Kicks" (2013)
"The Essential Book of Martial Arts Kicks" (2010) by Tuttle Publishing
"Le Grand Livre des Coups de Pied" (2018) by Budo Edition (in French)
"i Calci nelle Arti Marziali" (2015) by Edizioni Mediterranee (in Italian)
"Les Coups de Pied d'Arret" (2017) (in French)
"Les Coups de Pied Bas" (2016) (in French)
"Les Coups de Pied au Sol" (2018) (in French)

# DEDICATION

## To my First Grandson, Oliver

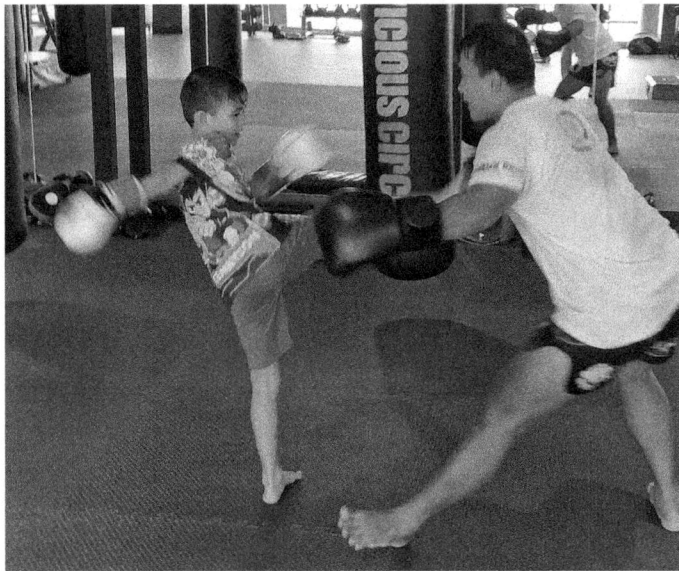

### The apple of my eye...

Dear Reader,

In this day and age, the life of a serious author has become quite difficult. The proliferation of books and the explosion of internet content has made it nearly impossible to promote work based on extensive research and requiring complex lay-out. Please enjoy this book. Once you are finished, I would ask kindly that you take a few short minutes to give your honest opinion. A unbiased Amazon review, of even a few words only, would be highly appreciated and encouraging.

Thank You,

*Marc*

**To practice five things under all circumstances constitutes perfect virtue; these five are gravity, generosity of soul, sincerity, earnestness, and kindness.**
**~Confucius**

# ACKNOWLEDGEMENTS

Aviva Giveoni

Without the active support of my wife and life companion, *Aviva Giveoni*, this book would not have come to life. Being an athlete in her own right, she understands the meaning of hard work and dedication.

Sensei Sydney Faige in action

Among many teachers and heads and shoulders above, my late Sensei, -*Sidney (Shlomo) Faige*-, should be mentioned with longing thankfulness. Sensei Faige founded the Shi-Heun style of Karate.

Roy and Marc

Special Thanks to my life-long friend and training partner, *Roy Faige*, for his help and support. Roy is now heading the Shi Heun school is also my co-author of *The Essential Book of Martial Arts Kicks*. His influence and advice is felt in nearly every page of this work and the previous books in the series.

Thank you to *Ziv Faige, Gil Faige, Shay Levy, Dotan De Bremaeker, Nimrod De Bremaeker and Itay Leibovitch* who helped by painstakingly posing for some of the photographs.

Dotan De Bremaeker

Most photographs have been taken by the author and Aviva Giveoni. But special thanks have to be extended to talented *Grace Wong* for some long sessions. Thank you also to professional photographer *Guli Cohen*: some of the photographs in this book have been extracted from the photo sessions he gracefully did for previous volumes.

The drawings in this book are mine. Everything that I have learned about line art, I have done so from professional Illustrator *Shahar Navot*, who illustrated *The Essential Book of Martial Arts Kicks*. Thanks Shahar!

## To expect bad men not to do wrong is madness.
## ~Marcus Aurelius

# CONTENTS

# Foreword to the "Kicks" Series

## A goal is not always meant to be reached, it often serves simply as something to aim at.
### ~Bruce Lee

*The 'Foreword' and 'General Introduction' are very similar to those of the previous book in the 'Kicks' series. In order to spare a near re-read to our faithful readers of 'Low Kicks', 'Stop Kicks', 'Ground Kicks', 'Stealth Kicks', 'Sacrifice Kicks and 'Krav Maga Kicks' we invite you to go directly to the 'Introduction to Joint Kicks' on page 20.*

My Martial Arts career started with Judo at age 6. Judo was pretty new Fifty years ago, and a bit mystical in the Western World. A mysterious Oriental Art teaching how to use one's opponent's strength against him was a pretty attractive proposition for a wimpy kid. And the decorum and costume trappings made it a unique selling proposition. That is, until the Kung Fu craze of the Seventies, starring Bruce Lee, and then others.

In my opinion, what fascinated the Western masses, and the teen-ager I was then, was mostly the fantastic kicking maneuvers in the spectacular fights of those Kung-Fu movies. The bulk of the fight scenes were based on spectacular exchanges, the likes of which we had never seen before. What was new and revolutionary back then, may seem banal and common to today's younger reader. But we had been raised in the era of boxing and we had been conditioned by the fair-play of *Queensburry's* rules: we had no idea one could fight *like that*!

It was also the first time that the general public in Europe and America had seen a well-rounded Martial Art in action: punching, but also striking, kicking, throwing down, grappling, locking... It comprised all fighting disciplines in seamless aggregation. Wow! Judo was great, but I now wanted to *kick* like Bruce Lee. I therefore took up *Shotokan Karate*. 'Shotokan-ryu' is not the most impressive kicking style, but it was then the most developed Kicking Art outside of Asia and the only one available to me. It is as well and I certainly do not regret it. Though it is not an art known for extravagant kicks, Shotokan is very well organized didactically. It also emphasizes tradition, hard training, focus (*Zanshin*) and mastery of basic work. In all athletic endeavors, the continuous drilling of basic work at all levels of proficiency is the only real secret to success.

Shotokan Karate drills and low training stances definitely fit this bill.

So, during the whole of my career, I kept practicing Shotokan Karate, or a Shotokan-derived style at all times. I also kept at Judo, my first love. But in parallel, I started to explore other Arts a few years at the time, as opportunities and geography allowed. During my long Martial Arts career, I also did practice assiduously Karatedo from the *Kyokushinkai, Shotokai, Wadoryu* and *Sankukai* schools. I also trained for long stints of *TaeKwonDo, Muay Thai, Krav Maga, Capoeira, Savate-Boxe Française*, two styles of traditional *Ju-Jitsu* and some soft styles of *Kung Fu*. This search is where I developed my individual methods and my own understanding of the Art of Kicking and its place in complex fighting. It also provided the basis on which to build my own personal research. Of course, this is strongly accented towards the type of maneuvers and training that favor my personal physiology and personality, but I have tried very hard to keep an open mind, among others through coaching.

Sometimes during this maybe too eclectic career, my travels took me to the **Shi-Heun** School of the late *Sensei Sidney Faige*, mentioned in the Acknowledgements. The *Shi-Heun* style is *Shotokan*-derived and mixed with *Judo* practice. It emphasizes extreme conditioning, total fighting under several realistic rules sets and the personal quest for what works best for oneself. And its self-defense training is based on no-nonsense

Sensei Sidney Faige

*Krav Maga*. As this was only the early Eighties, this was definitely a prophetic ancestor of today's phenomena of Mixed Martial Arts of 'UFC' fame. The free-fighting rules in the *Dojo* were 'all-out' and 'to-the-ground', but this did not hinder the success of the School's students in more traditional tournaments under milder rules. The direct disciples of *Sensei Faige* did indeed roam the tournament scene undefeated for years.

In these days, points tournament fighting was mainly WUKO (World Union of Karate Organizations), with some notable exceptions like *Kyokushinkai* and *Semi-contact Karate* bouts. Unfortunately, WUKO generally (boringly) consisted in two competitors safely jumping up-and-down and waiting for the other to initiate a move, in order to stop-reverse-punch him to the body.

Sensei Faige with the winning Israeli National Team; the author and Roy Faige are on the right

When my name was called up in these events, there was usually some spontaneous applause from the spectators; they knew they were going to see, finally, some kicking. I apologize if it sounds like boasting; the point I am trying to make is that Karate fans of these times came to see kicking and rich fighting moves, and not some unrealistic form of boxing. And this is not to denigrate *Karatedo*, but more the castrating effect of unintelligent rules sets.

Marc and Roy facing off at the finals of a 1987 Points Tournament

*Marc, kicking in point tournament*

It is my strong belief that Kicking is what made the Oriental Martial arts so appealing. As I have already mentioned in articles and previous books, I do firmly argue that **kicking is more effective than punching.** This usually causes many to stand up, disagree and maybe want to *punch* me. This is an old debate, still raging, and I respectfully ask to be allowed to complete the sentence. I strongly believe that kicking is more effective than punching, **but proficiency takes much more time and work**. When presented this way, I do hope that this opinion is more acceptable to most. Let me detail my position briefly.

### Kicking is more efficient than punching:

1. Because of the longer range

2. Because the muscles of the leg are much bigger and powerful than those of the arms

3. Because kicking targets, unlike punching targets, go from head all the way down to toes

4. Because kicks are less expected and therefore more surprising than punches, especially at shorter ranges

I readily admit that the opponents of my position do have valid arguments. They will point out that kicks are inherently slower than punches and can be easily jammed be-

*One needs to drill kicks from very close ranges as well*

cause they start from longer ranges. They will also point out that kicking often opens the groin, while forgetting that so does punching usually as well. It is my experience that, - **after a lot of dedicated and intelligent work-,** many kicks can be *as swift as punches and can be delivered at all ranges and from all positions.*

During all my training years, I invested a lot of time, personal drilling and original research into Kicking Arts from all over the world. I experimented with all training tips gathered and I endeavored to try all mastered new kick variations in actual free-fighting and competitive tournaments. Here is the place to note that this is *not* about a huge number of different techniques; it is about finding the best possible techniques suited to one's specific strength, physiology and affinities (Once you have found your few techniques and the best way to drill them, then you focus on fast and perfect execution from all ranges and positions). During my quest in the realm of kicking, I slowly developed a personal kicking style based on my personal history and mindset. I researched most of the available literature, but very few treatises were actually *dedicated* to kicking. The few works I found about kicking were generally very good, but usually style-restricted and unorganized. I never found the kind of book that I would have liked to have at the start of my Martial arts career. And so I decided to write it myself and share my global view of the subject. To the best of my knowledge, there has never been an attempt to compile and organize all the different Kick types and variation in such a way that it could serve as a reference work and the basis for exploration for the kick-lover. I did try to start this potentially huge work, probably imperfectly, with a series of Books I chose to name the 'Kicks series'. A global overview of Basic Kicks was presented in **'The Essential Book of Martial Arts Kicks'** (Tuttle). Its success lead me to follow with the important lower gates attacks in **'Low Kicks'**, and then **'Stop Kicks'** about preempting, jamming, impaling, obstructing and 'cutting' Kicks. As a sign of these MMA times, the series was naturally enriched by **'Ground Kicks'**. We continued this work with this, **'Stealth Kicks'**, covering misdirection and dissimulation while kicking; and went on to cover airborne and suicide-kicking with **'Sacrifice Kicks'**. No-nonsense practical kicking for Self-defense was covered in **'Krav Maga Kicks'**, and this book will concentrate on attacking the joints in order to destroy the opponent's ability to keep fighting. We hope that all this work will be built upon by others in the future. As mentioned and underlined many times, kicking proficiency requires a lot of serious drilling. I have therefore also published a work about the basic general drills that will help you reach higher levels of proficiency. As in all athletic endeavors, it is the basic drills that will build the strong foundation needed; and it is to those basic drills that the truly good athlete will come back for further progress again and again. **'Plyo-Flex Training for Explosive Martial Arts Kicks and Other Performance Sports'** does present those general, basic but so-important exercises that one should regularly practice for continuous improvement of kicking proficiency.

And now last, but certainly not least: it is important to underline that my strong views do not try in any way or form to denigrate the Punching Arts. My personal philosophy is that Martial arts are a whole with a world of possible emphasis. A complete Martial artist should be proficient in punching, kicking, moving, throwing, grappling, evading and more. An experienced Artist will have his own preferences and particular skills in his own way to look at the Martial Arts as a whole. And here must I add the obvious: *there is no kicking mastery* without punching proficiency! Even for a dedicated kicker, punching will be needed for closing the gap, feinting, setting up a kick, following it up and much more... This will be made abundantly clear from most of the applications presented in this volume, just as it is clear from all my previous work.

It must be said that Punching is sometimes the best or the only answer in some situations. I have known and met some extraordinary Punching Artists using kicks only as feints or set-ups. On the other hand, great kickers like legendary *Bill 'Superfoot' Wallace* were extremely skilled punchers and working hard at it, as I personally experienced in a few seminars. Kick and Punch, Punch and Kick: well-rounded is the secret.

And this leads me naturally to my last point. I would not want my books and my views to be misunderstood as an appeal to always kick when fighting, and especially not as an appeal to always high-kick. The best kicker in the world should not execute a high Kick, *just because he can*. A Kick should only be delivered *because and when it is suitable* to a specific situation! Obvious maybe, but certainly worth reminding. In someone else's words:

## Take things as they are. Punch when you have to punch. Kick when you have to kick.
### ~Bruce Lee

# GENERAL INTRODUCTION: THE 'KICKS' SERIES

This book is not a "How to" book for the beginner, but, hopefully, a reference work for the experienced Martial Artist. It presupposes the knowledge of stances, footwork, and concepts of centerline, guards, distance, evasions and more. It also expects from the reader a good technical level in his chosen Martial style, including kicking. As this work is building upon the *Essential* basic level towards more sophisticated kicking maneuvers, all *Essential Kicks* are considered mastered from the author's point of view. The reader is invited to consult previous work already mentioned above. This book is intended as a tool for self-exploration and research about kicking, outside experienced Artists' specific style. Therefore, the description of the different kicks is very short and typical examples are only briefly explained. The author relies more on photos and illustrations to exemplify his point. Let the reader try it and adapt it to his liking and morphology.

The author tends to prefer drawings over photographs to be able to underline salient points sometimes hidden in photos.

The experienced trainee will probably notice quickly that the basic background of the author is Japanese *Karate*. This cannot be avoided but was not deliberate. This book aspires to be as "style-less" as possible, as its purpose is to bridge across the different schools on the basis of common immutable principles. The author's philosophy is that Martial Arts are an interconnected whole, where styles are just interpretations of some principles and their adaptation to certain sets of strategies, rules, cultural constraints, or morphologies. It is one and same thing, although it may seem different from different angles. In the pictures and illustrations, the reader can see technical differences and adaptations from different styles. This is done on purpose to underscore the style-less philosophy of the treatise. Sometimes the foot of the standing leg is flat on the floor, as required in traditional Japanese styles, and sometimes the heel is up as in certain deliveries of Korean arts. It should be clear that the biomechanical principles are identical for trained artists and the small differences of emphasis are meaningless. It is more important for a trainee to adapt the technique to his morphology and preferences, once it is well mastered. This book definitely does not pretend to present an axiomatic way to kick! In the same vein, arms during kicking are sometimes close to the body in hermetic guard and sometimes loose and counterbalancing the kicking move. Hands can be open, or fists tight.

Like in previous efforts, it has proved very difficult to name and organize the kicks into and within groups. The author has given the techniques descriptive names in English, whenever possible commonly used names. But the more complex, exotic and hybrid kicks have sometimes either several different appellations in use or none, while being difficult to describe. The names the author has chosen could certainly be disputed and improved upon by some. For the most basic kicks common to all styles, we have added the respective original foreign names. The author apologizes in advance to the purists of all styles: It is clear that the description of a technique cannot be in all details valid for all styles (For example, the basic Front Kick is taught differently in *Shotokan* Karate than in *TaeKwonDo*). The original foreign names in Japanese, Korean, Chinese or Portuguese are just there as an indication for further research by the reader. It should also be noted that some techniques have different names in different schools of the same Art! For the more complex or exotic kicks, we have purposely omitted original names. Only when a kick is especially typical of a certain style, did we mention it, as a tribute to the specific school. The author also apologizes for his arbitrary transcription of foreign names, as purists could dispute the way it was done.

The kicks presented in this volume are tagged "Advanced". This does not necessarily mean that they are more difficult to execute than the *Essential* basic kicks. On the contrary. Besides being a requisite of some form of classification, it mainly means that the principles behind the "basic" kicks should be first thoroughly mastered. A *Front Stop Kick* is relatively easy to perform and slightly different than a regular Front Kick. But for maximum power, it is important to follow the same principles of a basic Front Kick, with chambering, kicking through and chamber back. And the principles of the leg development stay the same for the more difficult Flying Front Kick. And even if a Low Front kick seems easy to perform, it will be done so under the same principles already mastered for maximum speed and power. A typical Feint Kick, the Roundhouse-chambered Front Kick is slightly tricky to master, but it is more a question of hip flexibility and acquaintance drilling: the principles behind the power of what is ultimately a Front Kick stay the same. Once the principles behind the basic Front Kick are mastered, all other "Advanced" kicks will be faster and more powerful. **This is all about mastering the basics and principles first,** and only later trying out variations in all kinds of situations, fancier or not. This is, by the way, true for any other physical activity. But because Advanced Kicks are more a variation on the theme of their underlying basic kicks, they will be presented in all their complexity by many variations in specific applications.
*This* volume will not detail *Essential* basic kicks. If needed for the clarity of the narrative, some of them will be very briefly illustrated as a reminder.

This volume deals with **Ghost and Feint Kicks** only, as a variation of all six basic categories of Essential Kicks presented in previous work (Front, Side, Back, Roundhouse, Hook and Crescent Kicks).

Some Advanced Kicks have been omitted, as the author felt he had to draw the line somewhere. Again the decision was arbitrary, and could be considered as open for discussion. First have been omitted the whole range of nuances of a given kicks: As already mentioned, the same basic kicks are delivered in slightly different ways in all different styles and schools. The small differences come from the different emphasis of each style, and do not alter the basic principles. The author therefore described the kicks in the way his own experience dictates as best, and each reader can adapt it to his own personality. Many possible variations are presented for completeness in the applications though.

Secondly, hybrid kicks variations have been omitted, as the infinite number of intermediate possible deliveries in between two kicks would make this endeavor ridiculous. For example, many possible kicks as hybrids of Front and Roundhouse Kicks exist, each one with different levels of emphasis on the "front" side and the "roundhouse" side. In this specific book about Feint Kicks of all types, it is even truer: there are a great number of deliveries possibilities to execute a Roundhouse-chambered Front Kick, as the length and depth of the feinting part of the kick is highly dependent on the circumstances and the reaction of the opponent.

*Knee Strike*

Kicks combinations, and kick-punch combinations are infinite in numbers and will not be presented as such. Knee strikes, although very effective and versatile, will not be presented as such; for the purpose of this work, they will not be considered as kicks.

The remaining **Joint Kicks**, which will be presented in this work, will be so, generally, in a set descriptive way: After a brief **general** introduction and the **description** of the kick (mainly by illustrations), the main **key points** to remember for a good execution will be noted. Please remember that the book is intended for conversant martial artists. The relevant **targets** to be kicked in most applications will be mentioned. Examples of **typical application** will then be detailed and illustrated.

The typical application will generally be, unless irrelevant, a detailed use or set up of the given kick in a tournament-type situation. This will generally be a movements combination based on alternating different attack angles or/and levels (For example: hi-lo-hi, or/and outside/inside/outside), or the Progressive Indirect Attack principle as it is called by Jeet Kune Do artists. The tactical principle involved will not be detailed or presented systematically though, as it is beyond the scope of this volume. Of course, those applications will also usually be relevant to real life situation, and training work. Whenever possible, *specific training* tips to improve the given kick will be detailed. The specific training section will be brief and will only deal with the very specific characteristics of the kick and the ways to perfect them; general kick training guidelines are outside the scope of this book. The training of a Joint Kick is generally also the drilling of the corresponding Essential basic kicks, before the fusion of the two into the joint-targeting version. Back to basics then! Last, and in order to widen the scope of applications, an additional example of the use of the kick will be presented, generally more suitable to a *self-defense* or mixed martial arts application.

And now, let us go to JOINT KICKS...

## Victorious warriors win first and then go to war, while defeated warriors go to war first and then seek to win
## ~Sun Tzu

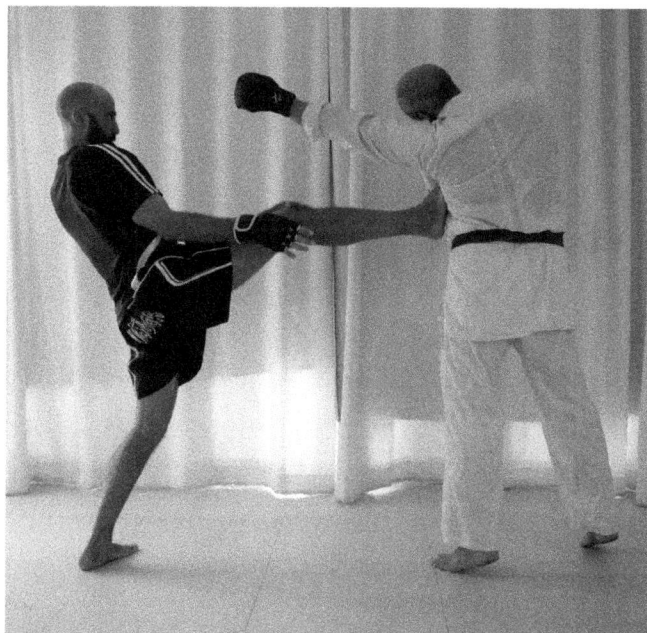

# Introduction to Joint Kicks

*Joint Kicks* are first and foremost Essential Kicks that we already know (as this book is aimed at proficient Martial Artists). They are simply targeting joints, and are sometimes executed slightly differently in order to ensure maximum joint damage.

A joint, or articulation, is defined as a structure in the human body at which two parts of the skeleton are fitted together. They are constructed to allow for different degrees and types of movement. For our purpose, we concentrate on the main joints of the four limbs, though there are many more joints in the human body. Those are: foot, knee, hip, hand and fingers, wrist, elbow and shoulder. To those we shall also add the neck joints with special techniques.

1.      **The Knee Joint** joins the thigh with the leg and consists of two articulations: one between the femur and the tibia, and one between the femur and the patella.  It is the largest joint in the human body and is classified as a modified "hinge joint", which permits flexion and extension as well as slight internal and external rotation. The knee joint and its ligaments  are extremely vulnerable to injury, as everybody knows or should know.

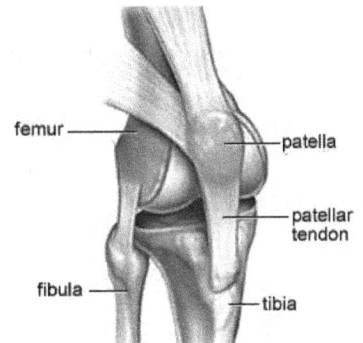

2.      **The Hip Joint** (or acetabulofemoral joint) joins the femur and the acetabulum of the pelvis. Its primary function is to support the weight of the body in both static and dynamic (e.g. walking) postures, and so this is the most important articulation in balance control. The hip joint is classified as a "synovial joint" formed by the articulation of the rounded head of the femur and the cup-like acetabulum of the pelvis. It forms the primary connection between the bones of the lower limb and the axial skeleton of the trunk and pelvis. Both joint surfaces are covered with a strong but lubricated layer called articular hyaline cartilage. The cuplike acetabulum forms at the joining of three pelvic bones — the ilium, pubis, and ischium. The hip joint is then reinforced by four ligaments.

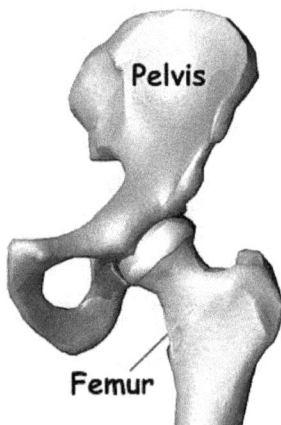

3.    __The Human Foot__ is a complex mechanical structure containing 26 bones, 33 joints (20 of which are actively articulated), and more than a hundred muscles, tendons, and ligaments. The main joints of the foot are the ankle, the subtalar joint and the interphalangeal articulations of the foot. The foot can be subdivided into the hindfoot, the midfoot, and the forefoot:

- The *hindfoot* is composed of the talus (or ankle bone) and the calcaneus (or heel bone). The two long bones of the lower leg, the tibia and fibula, are connected to the top of the talus to form the ankle. Connected to the talus at the subtalar joint, the calcaneus, the largest bone of the foot, is cushioned underneath by a layer of fat.
- The five irregular bones of the *midfoot*, the cuboid, navicular, and three cuneiform bones, form the arches of the foot which serves as a shock absorber. The midfoot is connected to the hind- and fore-foot by muscles and the sensitive plantar fascia.
- The *forefoot* is composed of five toes and the corresponding five proximal long bones forming the metatarsus. Similar to the fingers of the hand, the bones of the toes are called phalanges and the big toe has two phalanges while the other four toes have three phalanges. Both the midfoot and forefoot constitute the dorsum (the area facing upwards while standing) and the planum (the area facing downwards while standing). The instep is the arched part of the foot between the toes and the ankle.

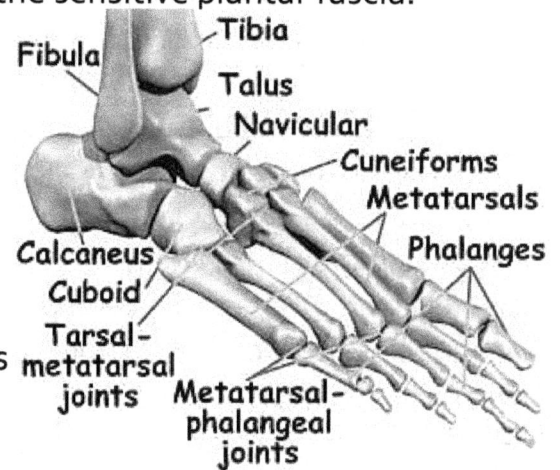

Lots of little joints waiting to be crushed...

4.    __The Human Hand__ comprises the wrist, the hand itself and the fingers. The Wrist Joint is generally defined as the carpus (or carpal bones), a complex of eight bones forming the proximal skeletal segment of the hand.

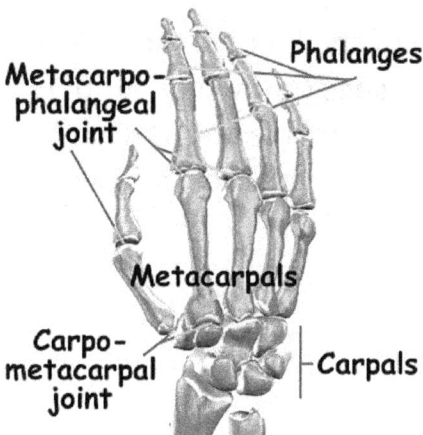

The hand joints are as follows: The carpometacarpal joint which connects the carpal bones to the metacarpal bones which are joined at the intermetacarpal articulations. In the fingers are the metacarpophalangeal joints (including the knuckles) between the metacarpal bones and the phalanges or finger bones which are interconnected by the interphalangeal joint. Again, lots of articulations to crush, with no need for overwhelming power...

5.     __The Elbow Joint__ is the ("synovial hinge") joint between the humerus in the upper arm and the radius and ulna in the forearm. It allows the hand to be moved towards and away from the body, which is critical in fighting. The elbow region includes prominent landmarks such as the sensitive *olecranon* (the bony prominence at the very tip of the elbow), the elbow pit, and the lateral and medial epicondyles . The elbow joint has three different portions surrounded by a common joint capsule. These are joints between the **three** bones of the elbow, the humerus of the upper arm, and the radius and the ulna of the forearm. The elbow, like other joints, has ligaments on either side that impose strict limitations on abduction, adduction, and axial rotation. Those limitations are what your kicks are supposed to force through in order to cause damage.

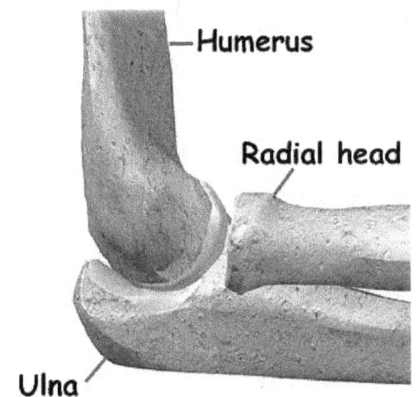

6.     __The Shoulder Joint__ is a very complex and sensitive articulation. The *sternoclavicular joint* links the sternum and the clavicle, ans is considered by Martial Artists as part of the shoulder. It is composed of two portions separated by fibrocartilage. The bone areas entering into its formation are the sternal end of the clavicle, the upper and lateral part of the sternum and the cartilage of the first rib. The articular surface of the clavicle is much larger than that of the sternum, and is covered with a layer of cartilage, which is considerably thicker than that on the sternum. The *shoulder joint* itself (in fact, the glenohumeral joint) is a multiaxial 'ball and socket' joint which involves articulation between the glenoid cavity of the scapula (shoulder blade) and the head of the humerus (upper arm bone). *Due to the very loose joint capsule, it is the most mobile joint of the human body, but also very sensitive to stress.* The socket of the glenoid cavity of the scapula contains a ring of cartilaginous fibre attached to the circumference of the cavity, and this ring is continuous with the tendon of the biceps. Moreover, a number of small fluid-filled sacs (known as synovial bursae)are located around the capsule to aid mobility. All this makes the shoulder joint extremely sensitive to injury.

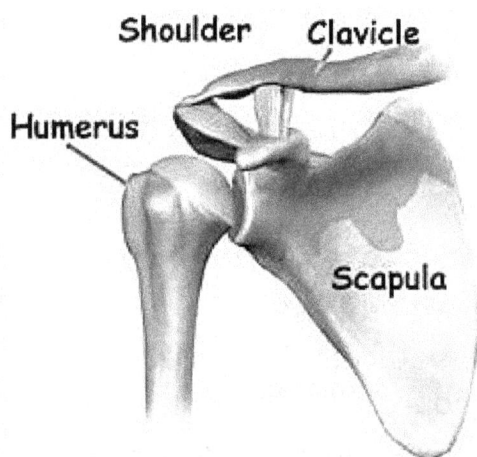

Most *Joint Kicks* are definitely out of the scope of competitive sports. They are more relevant to traditional Martial Arts study or to Self-defense applications, as they usually can provoke extremely serious damage. A damaged joint is, of course, very serious, completely disabling; and it usually can never be fully fixed. If you can hurt an assailant's joints early in a <u>real</u> fight, it goes without saying that he will be at your mercy.

This is the stuff of the traditional Martial Arts of old, destined for use on the battlefield. In previous books of this series, I have already hinted at the need to have such dangerous techniques in your arsenal. As mentioned there, *pain is not always enough to stop an attacker or to deter him*. Even a full-powered kick in the testicles is not always enough to stop an assailant. Some people are nearly impervious to pain; some people are highly trained to resist pain; some people have been through so much that it will not stop them; some assailants can be high on drugs, intoxicated or mentally unbalanced [I have seen such a situation with my own eyes at a public event: five highly trained and very strong security personnel unable to control an unbalanced individual with powerful blows]. The only two way to deal with an assailant that pain will not deter are: **Limb Destructions** and Chokes. The important Art of Choking (*Shime Waza*) is not relevant to our present subject; it requires serious training and extreme caution and has its advantages and disadvantages (one of which is the problematic dealing with several attackers). We are here left with the "Limb Destruction" that is basically the subject of this book. If you damage the elbow of an attacker, he will not be able to punch you, at least with this arm. If you damage an assailant's knee, he will not be able to move effectively towards you. If you crush an armed robber's fingers, he will not be able to hold his knife or pull his trigger. I think the point is clear and self-evident. It is, though, easily overlooked: how easy is it to stomp on an opponent's toes or fingers, and how much true damage can be achieved! And still these moves are too seldom drilled and used.

The late *Bruce Lee* was a proponent of attacks to the knee, emphasizing that a child has enough power to disable a strong adult by kicking his knee joint.

But this only emphasizes the need for ***very careful training and for self-control in all situations.***

Many Joint Kicks are simple basic Kicks directed at the joints. We have met them before in previous volumes of this work, and we will recall some of them in this book. We could mention: most of the Low Kicks, the Crescent Kicks to the elbows, the Downward Heel Kicks, the 'Low Kick' (Straight-leg Roundhouse) to the knee, the Upward Front and Upward Side Kicks, the Stomp Kicks on the fingers or feet, and many more. Here follow a few photographic examples, but the interested reader is invited to refer to the previous volumes for more. The other Kicks that will be presented in this volume are either more complex, or very specific, or exclusively joint-related.

Upward Side kick to the armpit

Crescent Kick to elbow

Low Soccer front kick to the knee

Stomp Kick to the ankle

Upward Front kick to the armpit

Stomping Low Front Kick to the knee

'Low Kick' to
the side knee

Stomp Kick
to wrist and/
or fingers

<u>Low Kicks</u> are often *Joint Kick*s when targeting the knee. We shall present advanced and sophisticated kicks, but it is good to remember that the simple things are often the ones that work best. A simple, direct and fast straight kick to the knee joint is very easy to succeed with, but it can also be extremely damaging. You should remember two things though: **1**. Always kick *through* into the knee, and **2**. Keep your *upper body as immobile as possible* in order to avoid detection (as explained in 'Stealth Kicks'). The Drawings below illustrate how to execute the simple Low Front Kick *stealthily*.

*Keep the upper body as immobile as possible for a fast and stealthy delivery of the Low Front Kick to the forward knee*

Another set of kicks with joint-damaging properties are the <u>Stop Kicks</u> aiming at the kicking legs of the opponent in motion towards you. By kicking powerfully the shins or knees of a leg coming towards you with its own strong momentum, you send radiating energy to all the joints of said leg, all the way to the hip. The examples illustrated at the top of next page could therefore be considered *Joint Kicks* as well as Stop Kicks.

➡

A few examples of painful 'Stop-the-leg' Stop Kicks that can also damage the joints

And now, a note of caution:

**Joint Kicks** are not for sport or for games. They are very serious and debilitating attacks to be used only in real self-defense situations and in a manner proportional to the seriousness of the threat.

Try to imagine having no clue of what transpired before, but seeing someone crushing somebody else's fingers with intent, or kicking his knee out brutally and visibly purposely. You would be appalled, shocked, disgusted. You would also probably hasten to pass judgement.

Just remember that you could be in a situation in which to *have to* do these things to protect yourself or your loved ones from a vicious predator. And it could look bad...

On top of the obvious moral choices one has to make, one also has to take into account how things can look to an outside observer.

Ethically, the reader, who is a Martial Artist, should make sure he does everything to avoid a confrontation. If he is left no choice, he should make sure to defend himself in a way that is proportional and causes the minimum damage necessary to stop the engagement.

But sometimes, the minimum damage can still have to be serious. It could be a destructive Joint Kick necessary to neutralize an aggressor who does not relent otherwise. In that case, you should also think about the legal ramifications, and not only about the ethical ones.

_When executing a Joint Kick in a self-defense situation, you should carefully consider both the ethical and the legal aspects: Are you justified in causing serious bodily harm to your aggressor in this situation? In fact, you could rephrase this: Would a judge or a jury consider your action necessary to safeguard your own safety or that of others, or could you just have left the scene or taken less brutal action with no danger? And take into account that purposely attacking a joint, or stomping the fingers or the ankle of a downed opponent will look to any witness as brutal and going against every ingrained fair-play sense of normative citizens._

_It is more important to be wise than to be right...._

**There's only one basic principle of self-defense: you must apply the most effective weapon, as soon as possible, to the most vulnerable target.**
**~Bruce Lee**

# The Kicks

## 1. THE LOW FLYING SIDE KICK

### General

This is simply a Flying Side Kick to the joints of the hip or of the knee. The **Low Flying Side Kick** has already been presented in our book about *Sacrifice Kicks*, and the reader is invited to refer to it for more context. The Kick presented here specifically target joints and attacks them downwards from above with the full body weight being added to the momentum and to the powerful leg extension. This is an extremely dangerous kick, and caution is warranted in training and in use.

*Low Flying Downward Side Kick to the knee*

### Description

The Low Flying Side Kick having been presented already, we shall describe it here in an applied form, as the natural extension of the Flying Stop-backfist maneuver. The "Timing" Stop-backfist-maneuver was once very popular in tournament circles as a safe scoring technique against an attacking opponent: you would jump into a long Backfist strike to the head of the opponent at the first hint of his starting an attack. The jump would 'protect' your lower body from the start of a kick or a sweep, and your chambering airborne did provide your trunk some protection from punches. It should be noted that this technique is also very effective in real combat, especially in tandem with this Low Flying Side Kick.

The illustrations, at the top of next page, show how you jump up and forwards as soon as your opponent starts his attack. You backfist his face at the apex of your jump, and deliver a Flying Side Kick to his knee while starting your descent. Kick *through* the knee, with all your weight and momentum. Follow up, if needed.

➡

*Preemptive Flying Backfist to Downward Flying Side Kick*

*The Flying Stop Backfist*

## Key Points

- Jump high and *forward*.
- Jump with *knees as close to the chest* as possible, for protection and chambering.
- Kick *through* the target and reception yourself on the other foot.

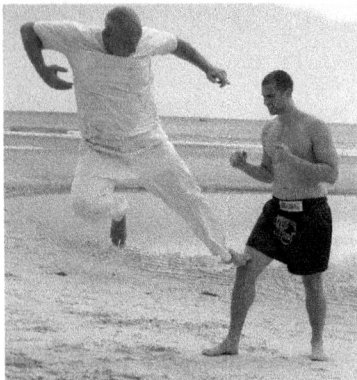

*Another Low Flying Side Kick to Knee joint*

## Targets

From the hip to the knee, hitting from above downwards. The Drawing and Photo illustrate the delivery to the hip joint.

*Attacking the Hip Joint from above*

*Flying Low Side Kick to the Hip Joint*

## 2. THE SIDE STOMP KICK BEHIND THE KNEE AND RELATED TECHNIQUES

### General

This is the probably the most classic of the Joint Kicks, used in all Martial Arts, from Old Ju jitsu to modern Krav Maga. It is easy to perform and difficult to fail with, while being tremendously effective. It is also a Kick that can be applied in a more controlled way if so wished, doing then less damage while still effectively neutralizing an opponent. The Kick has already been described in our book about *Low Kicks* and the reader is invited to refer to the relevant section for more context.

*The Side Stomp Kick behind the knee is much used in **Krav Maga***

### Description

The Figures show the delivery from the out-side of the opponent. It is a very basic Low Penetrating Side Kick (*Fumikomi- Karatedo*), but you do not chamber back *before you have kicked down through the opponent's knee and drilled it into the floor.*

**Fumikomi** *from the opponent's outside*

## Key Points

- Kick *through* the knee until it gets to the floor
- Do not chamber back *before you have stomped the knee to the floor.*
- Put the whole *body weight* into the Kick.
- This particular Kick is only applicable if you target the back of the knee: It is only possible if you are behind or on your opponent's out-side. You can also attack an opponent in front of you if he stands in a side guard, and you then deliver a *Curved Side Kick* to catch it on the side and slightly behind; see Photos below.

*Curved Side Kick from the front, to Stomping Side Kick*

## Target

The back of the knee, extended to the sides if the Kick comes from an oblique direction.

## Typical Applications

The Figures show a classic application of the Kick against a rear-leg Side Kick. The use of this technique against the standing leg of a kicking opponent (*Cutting Kick*) multiplies the damage to the joint, as it will cause a stronger fall onto the knee. In this example, you evade forwards and out (the rear-leg Side Kick) and immediately stomp-kick the back of his standing knee.

*Side Stomp Kick to back knee after evading a kicking attack*

**Remember that this Kick should be nearly automatic if you find yourself behind your opponent!** The coming Illustrations show the Kick as a follow-up to a high Roundhouse delivered from the out-side. This is a very effective *typical combination*, and a classic must-practice. You evade out a full-stepped Lunge Punch and deliver a nearly simultaneous high Roundhouse Kick. You chamber back the leg and, without lowering the foot to the ground, you stomp-kick the back of his knee in a continuous flowing move. After you have crushed his knee to the floor, you can switch legs and roundhouse-kick (or downward-roundhouse) the back of his neck.

*From high Roundhouse to back-of-the-knee Stomp*

## Self defense

This is a very important Kick for self-defense, as it is easy and tremendously effective. It allows an instant and full neutralization of an opponent. A crushed knee will seriously hamper even the most serious of assailants. It is a bread-and-butter kick in the no-nonsense Art of Krav Maga; and that says it all.

The Drawings show how to evade out and forward, with a full side-step, a straight and committed poking knife attack. You control the knife hand while immediately attacking the throat, with a Ridge-hand Strike for example. Keep a squeezing control of his throat and stomp the back of his knee. To follow up, you could first chamber back and then crush his ankle.

1

*The Kick of choice when you evade out*

4          5          6

*THE SIDE STOMP KICK BEHIND THE KNEE*    33

The next series of Photos illustrates the same evading-out against a Downward Overhead Strike; it could be a Stick or a Knife Strike, or simply an unarmed Haywire punching attack. You evade out while controlling the attacking arm, and stomp the back of the knee. Of course, follow up.

*Evade Overhead Strike to the outside and ... stomp!*

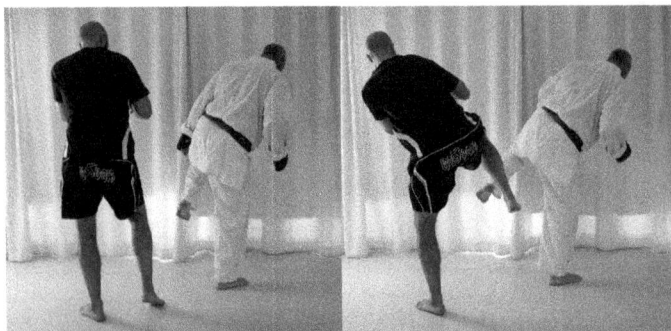

We shall now add another set of Photos illustrating the Stomping Kick after evading a Kick on the outside of the attacker. This technique should be use quasi-automatically if you find yourself at the back of the opponent.

*When you 'own' the opponent's back, stomp his knee and grind it into the floor*

And we shall follow with two simple Stop-kicking combinations. The Illustrations below show how you stop a Jabbing opponent with a well-timed high Roundhouse Stop Kick. Lower your kicking foot deep behind the attacker and spin-back while passing below his arm (if still extended). Your Spin-back Stomping Side kick will crush his knee to the ground, from behind.

*Roundhouse Stop Kick followed by Spin-back Side Stomp Kick to the back of the knee*

Our second example is based on a Soccer Low Front Stop Kick; and your opponent is a frequent user of the rear-leg Penetrating Front Kick. Once you have ascertained that, it will be easy to strike his incoming shin with a powerful rear-leg Soccer Stop Kick.

As he lands forward, you pull back the foot while controlling his hands, and execute immediately a (Hopping) front-leg Stomping Side Kick to the back of his landing knee. As he crumbles back, finish him off with a Forearm Strike to the face or the throat.

*Soccer Stop Kick to the shin of an incoming leg can be followed by a Side Stomp of the landing knee*

Another way to set up the Kick is to lure the opponent into a kicking attack by opening an obvious target; you can then evade the kick and stomp the landing knee. The Figures at the top of next page illustrate 'inviting' the opponent to attack with a Penetrating Front Kick that will be easily evaded forward/out. Block/control the incoming leg while already chambering the Stomp. Crush his landing knee into the ground.

*Cause or expect a Front Kick to evade, and stomp the back of the landing knee*

The coming combination is an interesting 'Destruction Series' starting from very close. Its purpose is to completely damage the knee joint of the opponent in order to neutralize him for good and prevent a continuation of the fight. From a Judo grip or even a Clinch, you attack the opponent's knee with a short Outside Hook Low Kick. Kick hard and well *into* the target, and immediately straighten your leg to hit the side of his knee with your thigh and force him to bend. As he bends, knee down with all your body weight onto his ankle. Stand up at once and use the same leg for a powerful Stomping Kick to the back of the same knee, as you 'own' his back.

*A destruction series against knee and ankle*

Of course, the simple Side Kick to the knee of a standing leg (*Cutting Kick*) will always work if you kick <u>through</u> the knee, regardless of the point of impact, be it front, side or back. The examples below show powerful rear-leg versions against a high Roundhouse Kick. You can either block (and lift) or simply evade. See Illustrations here and at the top of next page.

*Evade a high Roundhouse while blocking and rear-leg side-kick the standing knee*

*You can also simply duck low and simply evade the Kick before executing the Cutting Side Kick*

A classic way to drill the *Stomping Side Kick to the knee* is presented below; the Kick strikes the side of the knee in a way that will make it buckle. The opponent attacks with a lunging Reverse Punch that you evade and control. Switch hands to grab the punching arm and pull it forward, while chambering the Side Kick. As you have evaded out, you are in perfect diagonal position to kick the knee on which you pull his weight. Kick *through* in a stomping and slightly hooking way. This is a simple but important drill.

*Classic evade and side-kick the front knee*

# Don't fear failure. Not failure, but low aim, is the crime. In great attempts it is glorious even to fail.
## ~Bruce Lee

# 3. THE FRONT SIDE STOMP KICK

## General

This is the same Low Side Kick attack as previously, but this time to the front of the knee joint. We have already met this Kick in previous work (*Low Kicks*); but, here, it is presented specifically for attacks on the knee. Unlike the previous Stomp Kick to the back of the knee, you do not have to kick down all the way to the floor. You kick through the target though, and the damage will be done well before you reach the floor. In Japanese Karate, this Kick is called *Fumikiri* if delivered with the foot blade and *Fumikomi* if delivered with the plant of the foot.

*The Front Side Stomp Kick*

## Description

As shown in the Figures, this is a simple Side Kick delivered from full high chamber, down onto the front of the knee. After kicking *through* the target, you chamber back.

*It is in fact a regular Low Side Kick*

*The Front Side Stomp Kick to the knee*

## Key Points

- This is a regular Side Kick: *push the hips* into the Kick.
- *Chamber* high and fully!
- *Chamber back.*

## Targets

Aim for the higher part of the knee joint, so as to straighten his leg as you kick down.

## Typical Application

Many applications of this Kick have been presented in 'Low Kicks'. Here, we shall present the ideal opportunity for it: Attacking the knee of a landing kicking leg! This is a devastating counter after a "back & fro" evasion of a Front Kick. As shown in the Drawings, you evade your assailant's rear leg Front Kick by retreating *just* enough, while chambering the front leg in a regular Side Kick Chamber. As your overextended opponent lands forward, you deliver the Side Stomp Kick to the knee, thus straightening his leg and hurting the joint as his weight switches to the leg. Practice carefully, this is a very dangerous technique.

*Evade rearwards and kick the knee of the landing kicking leg*

## Specific Training

As you have to kick *through* and chamber *back*, it is an important Kick to practice on a heavy bag or an old tire hold by a partner (See Illustration).

*Drill the penetration of the Kick on a bag hold by a partner*

## Self defense

We have chosen to first illustrate the application of the Kick in a 3-levels kicking combination. As shown by the Drawings, you will use the momentum of a high kick for a full chamber to a deriving powerful knee Stomp. In our example, you take the initiative with a front-leg Roundhouse towards your assailant's groin. As he has to block or at least to react to the Kick, you smoothly turn it into a high Upward Front Kick towards his chin. Without lowering the foot, you chamber back into a Chamber, from which you deliver the *Side Stomp Kick to his front knee*. Follow up with a 'Low Kick' to his damaged knee. This combination is a fantastic drill for overall kicking proficiency, for hip flexibility and for learning to always vary the height of subsequent attacks.

*Triple Kick Combination ending in the opponent's knee destruction*

3          4          5          6

Our next example of the applied Stomp Kick is following a preemptive groin Kick against a threatening opponent armed with a knife or any other cold weapon. The assailant expects you to cower away, but you foil his expectations and surprise him by launching an aggressive and fast Hopping Body-bent Roundhouse Kick to his groin. You immediately follow up with a *Penetrating Side Kick through the front of his knee*. Keep attacking aggressively, for example with a high Backfist and a hard kicking Takedown. Once he is on the ground, you should try to stomp his fingers or/and ankles to neutralize him for further aggression. Note again the mid/low/hi/low pattern. See the Photos series at the top of next page.

*Crippling Knee Kick after a groin Roundhouse in Self-defense*

And now, we are presenting a *Krav Maga* sequence against an assailant rushing you in order to grab you or to strangle you. The *Side Kick to the front knee* will be used as a very effective Stop Kick, as you catch it in the midst of your opponent's step forward. The follow up is vintage Krav Maga: Downward Forearm Strike to the back of the neck, and Knee Strikes to the lower ribs and then to the face. And it is not necessarily over.

*The Knee Side Kick as a Stop Kick against an assailant coming towards you*

In the coming Photos, we are going to illustrate the use of the Kick as a naturally-flowing follow-up to a Roundhouse Kick. The first set of Photos shows the Stomping Kick after a Roundhouse Joint Kick to the inside knee; and the second set illustrates the same combination, but with the starting Roundhouse Kick targeting the groin.

*Kick the knee joint twice: Roundhouse and naturally-following Side Stomp Kick*

*Kick the opponent's groin and let it flow into a Side Stomp Kick to the knee*

The next Photos will now illustrate one of the best applications for this effective Kick: attacking the knee of a *landing kicking leg*. In our example, you evade rearwards a Front Kick just far enough not to be touched, and you stomp-kick the knee of the attacker's leg as it lands forward.

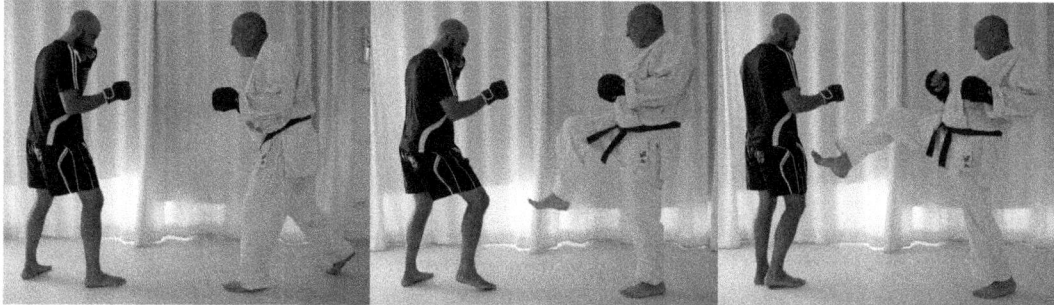

*Stomp the front knee of a kicking leg, just as it lands!*

The next Drawings show another 'landing' application, but this time, the landing comes *after* you have stop-kicked the opponent's developing Front Kick ('Stop-the-kick' technique – see *Stop Kicks*). The Stop Kick already causes some knee joint damage, as it comes full power into collision with a full powered chambering kick. And then ...

*Soccer Low Front Kick to the shin of a developing Front Kick, turns naturally into a Side Stomp Kick of the landing leg*

The Drawings at the top of next page illustrate the stealthy delivery of the Kick to the forward knee of your opponent. The key to success is to *keep the upper body immobile* in order to prevent early detection. You then extend the kicking leg forward until you reach the opponent's knee level. The trajectory then switches to sideways and hooks slightly forward in order to make the knee buckle. From then on, stomp in "Side Kick-mode" to crush his knee to the ground.

➡️

*The stealthy delivery of the Forward Side Stomp Kick to the knee; fast and sneaky*

**Be yourself; everyone else is already taken.**
**~Oscar Wilde**

# 4. THE FRONT SOCCER STOMP KICK

## General

This is, of course the Joint Kick version of the *Outward-tilted Front Kick* described in

'The Essential Book of Martial Arts Kicks' and also mentioned in' Low Kicks'. It can target the front or the back of the knee joint, **in a stomping movement**. In that, it is similar to the previously presented Low Side Stomp Kick (See Chapter 2). Again, it is a tremendously effective Kick, versatile and easy to perform, and very typical of many *Kung Fu* styles.

*The Front Soccer Stomp Kick to the back of the knee*

## Description

The Figures show the (less common) use of the Kick against *the front of the knee joint,* and with a hand feint to facilitate the stealthy delivery. Attacking the front knee requires more power and will usually be performed as a rear-leg Kick. In the example, you jab towards your opponent's eyes while simultaneously chambering the rear leg in a high typical Front Kick Chamber. Stomp down on the knee joint in a move that attempts to straighten your opponent's leg as it strikes *through* the knee.

*Chamber high and stomp down through the knee*

## Key Points

- *Chamber high* for a powerful Stomp. Remember that in your opponent's mind, a high Chamber usually means a high kick, not a low one.
- Tilt the foot *while going down*; there is no need to telegraph your move.
- Kick *through* the target. In the case of a back-of-the-knee kick, stomp until the knee gets crushed into the floor. In the case of a front-of-the-knee Kick, make sure you cause a straightening of his leg.

Chamber high to stomp low and through

Kick through

Aim at causing the straightening of his leg

## Targets

The knee joint from all sides.
Of course, if your opponent is on the floor or on his hands and knees, you can stomp the fingers, wrists, ankles and more.

## Typical Applications

The following Drawings show a very classic *offensive* move leading to full stomping of the back of the knee. You start by delivering a full-powered Sweep to the front foot of the opponent, in order to put him off-balance and place yourself on his blind out-side. As he reacts naturally and probably jabs (or backfists), you will block and get hold of his front hand while already chambering the rear leg. Nearly simultaneously, use your other hand to deliver a Palm Strike to the side of his head before reaching to catch his shoulder. Stomp the back of his knee, all the way down, before following up.

*A powerful Sweep will place you right for the Soccer Stomp Kick*

The coming Photos underline the fact that the Kick can and should be delivered as well to the side of the knee if the opportunity arises. In our example, you evade a punch to the inside of the opponent and stomp the inside knee. Simple, fast and devastating.

*Evade in and crush the inside knee*

The Figures at the top of next page will show a more sophisticated use of the Kick, typical of *Kung Fu* styles like *Wing Chun*. Get control your opponent's front hand by pushing it against his own body. All the while you are placing your front knee *outside* his, but you keep your ankle *inside* his. By pushing forward and in, you will buckle and control his front leg. Immediately chamber up the rear leg to stomp the back of his buckled knee. Follow up, for example by grabbing his hair and pulling his head back to offer his throat to a Hand-blade Strike.

➤

*Wing Chung Knee Control to back-of-the-knee Stomp*

## Self defense

The following Illustrations show a very simple but effective use of the Kick against an attempted Shoulder (*Ippon Soei Nage*) or Hip Throw (*O Goshi*). It is presented from a traditional Judo grip starting position (*Kumi Kata*). As soon as your opponent gives you his back to set up the takedown, you stomp the back of his knee! And then push him to the ground...

*Fast and easy against an attempted Shoulder Throw*

Our next application will illustrate the Kick in the middle of a string of techniques following the 'blocking and diverting' of a kicking attack by your assailant. You simply evade and redirect a mid-body Roundhouse attack to place yourself on your off-balanced opponent's blind side.

→

... Follow up with a 'Joint Low Kick' to the knee of the *landing leg*. Kick hard and through to damage the joint. You land deep with your kicking leg and chamber the other leg, now completely behind the attacker. Stomp the back of the same injured knee and catch his head to pull it rearwards and down; you can simply hold the head, or grab the hair or the ears. Pull the head down to meet with a rebounding Knee Strike. You can then use the head to push the assailant violently to the ground, head first. **<u>This is a dangerous technique and extreme caution is required in training!</u>**

*Stomp after an evasion and a 'Low Kick' get you in the opponent's back; follow-up resolutely*

But before we leave the Soccer Kick, it is important to remind the reader that the simplest techniques are often the most effective. Not always is the stomping version of the Soccer Low Front Kick necessary. The coming Illustrations, at the top of next page, show how to deal with a classic Stepping Punch move, with an exceedingly simple maneuver. Evade forward and out, control the incoming arm, and soccer-kick the joint knee of the incoming leg. Easy, fast and painful. Follow up of course...

➡

*An applied simple regular Soccer kick to the knee*

But if you can stomp, all the better! The coming set of Drawings illustrate a traditional drill. An evading Outside Block of a Stepping Punch can become a perfect position for a Cross Step and the stomping of the rear leg of the opponent. This is an excellent drill for general kicking mastery.

*Applied Front Soccer Front Kick to the back of the knee of the rear leg of a punching attacker*

We shall now follow with a traditional *Kung Fu* drill that emphasizes that pulling the opponent towards you while kicking him will also add to the destructive effect. In our example, you block a High Reverse Punch with your rear hand and grab the attacking wrist. Pull while countering with a front-hand Punch to the exposed armpit/high ribs. Your punching hand grabs the opponent's upper arm so that you can pull him in with both hands while kick-stomping his upper leg between the knee and the hip for damage to both.

*Pull the opponent in as you stomp kick his knee or hip*

We are now going to present a very different stomping technique, but still close to a Front Soccer Kick. It is basically a *Flying Stomp Kick* targeting the ankle or the top of the foot. The damage to the ankle and foot joints from landing on them with a kick and all your body weight is pretty clear. The maneuver in itself is an overwhelming committed jump towards the opponent with both feet and both fists. No matter what connects or not: the purpose is to fool him and land with a Stomping Kick onto his ankle.

*No coming back: jump at the opponent with feet and fists and land on his ankle*

And another variation of the Front Stomping Kick is presented below. It is different in its principles, but the execution is that of a high Stomping Front Kick. This technique is a simple Leg Block, or '**Kick-the-leg**' Stop Kick, against a standard all-in Low Kick. It is simple to understand and the combined power of both kicks make it very hard on the opponent's knee joint. See drawings below.

*Front Stomping high Stop Kick against Low Kick*

A further variation of the previous version would be to stop-kick *the hip joint*. In the example illustrated at the top of next page, the Stop Kick is in itself the start of a '<u>**Climbing Technique**</u>' (*More on East-Asian Climbing Techniques further in the text*). You use the struck hip joint as a ladder for a very surprising Flying Knee Strike to the chin. This overwhelming stopping maneuver is very efficient and surprisingly easy to succeed with. Just drill, and then dare!

➤

*Front Stomping Stop Kick to the hip becomes a Climbing Knee Strike*

The Stomping Kick at the back of the opponent's knee is also highly recommended when you can place your opponent in a *standing Rear Naked Choke*; it will place him totally off-balance and place him fully in your control. Even better, if you want to take him to the ground to finish him there...

In the Drawings below, we have illustrated a classic traditional exercise: you evade forward and out a downward stick (or sword) strike and you push the attacker's arms down. Keep lunging to the opponent's back while striking his throat with your forearm. The Strike becomes a Rear Naked Choke and you immediately stomp the back of his knee to hurt, mollify and better control him.

*Use the Stomp Kick to the back of an opponent's knee after you have set a Rear Naked Choke*

Of course, the Kick is ideal when it is the opponent that places himself in front of you by himself, for example, in order to set-up a 'come-along Armlock'. The Illustrations, at the top of next page, show how the opponent grabs your wrist and encircles your elbow with the other arm in order to set up a classic Armlock. Immediately twist your arm (thumb down) in order to place your elbow joint sideways and not too susceptible to the fulcrum of the Lock. Simultaneously, chamber the Soccer Stomp Kick. Stomp violently all the way to the floor, and attack his eyes with your free hand. It will then be easy to free your locked arm and follow up.

➤

*The Stomp Kick as a counter to a classic Come-along Armlock*

# Use only that which works, and take it from any place you can find it.
## ~Bruce Lee

# 5. THE LOW ROUNDHOUSE TO THE BACK OF THE KNEE

*O Mawashi Barai (Karatedo)*

## General

This is a variation of the Low Roundhouse Kick, exclusively delivered to the side of the knee (inside or outside) and with a forward hooking motion designed to make the leg buckle. Not only does it get the opponent on his knee, but it also causes a lot of joint damage. This technique is relatively typical to the *Sankukai Karate* style and of some *Silat* Arts

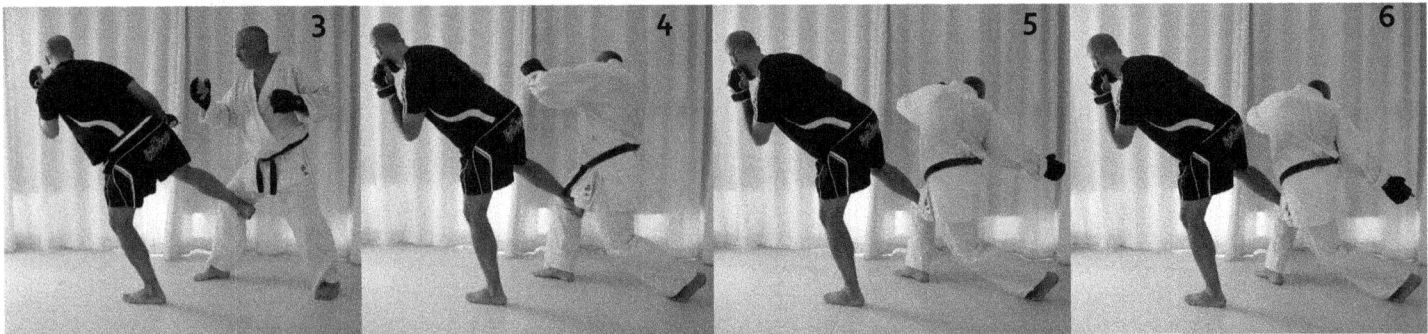

*O Mawashi Barai*

## Description

As it is not really a static kick, we shall directly describe an Application. The Figures below show how you evade backwards and control a full-step Lunge Punch, to immediately launch a rear-leg Roundhouse Kick through the side of his front knee. As you connect, you hook inside the knee and "round" the trajectory of the Kick towards the front of your opponent's knee. As his front leg buckles and he falls on his back knee, you deliver a hook punch to the side of his head. Follow up.

Applied 'O Mawashi Barai' to the knee of an opponent stepping in with a punch

## Key Points

- The *circular trajectory* is key to the success of the "buckling" technique.
- It is critical to kick *through* the knee.

## Specific Training

- Kick *inside a tire* hold by a partner. Make sure to hook in and forward (See Figure). The purpose is to try to take the tire away from the partner holding it.
- Drill with a *partner*, slowly and carefully to avoid joint damage. Make sure he feels the buckling of the leg.

*Drilling the Kick with an old car tire*

## Self defense

The next example illustrates an application of the Kick to the outside knee. The principle stays the same: hook in and forwards. In opposite stances, you evade out a jab, block up and get control the hand; simultaneously you are delivering a rear leg Roundhouse to his head. Lower the leg directly into a Downward Side Kick to his front knee. Lower the leg to the floor, pivot and get hold of his lead shoulder as well, as you deliver a full-powered rear-leg Roundhouse Kick to the outside of his front knee.

*Hook in and forward.* Follow up as he goes down, for example by keeping hold of his wrist to stomp his armpit as he lands.

*Buckling Kick on the outside knee to take the attacker down after softening him up*

4          5          6          7

The next series of Photos illustrates a natural same-leg Hook Kick follow-up to the Buckling Kick: you can easily kick his head, even if you are not flexible!

*Buckling Low Roundhouse to the Back of the Knee, followed by a same-leg returning Hook kick to the face*

And the last series of self-explaining Photos illustrates another follow-up for this off-balancing Kick: A Knee Strike. The set shows two knee kicks in series, with the second one 'hooking'.

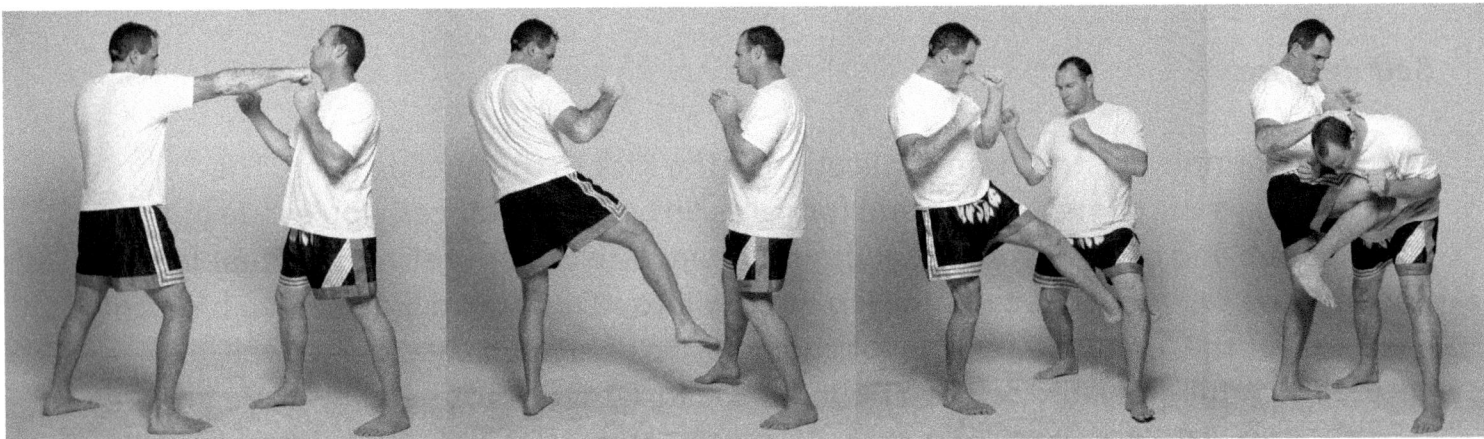

*Jab, front-leg Kick to the forward knee, rear-leg Buckling Kick to the other Knee, Knee Strike*

We shall now follow with special techniques from the same general family. *The first one* is applied from the ground. In the Illustrations at the top of next page, you see how to block and redirect a kick from a standing opponent, in order to 'get' his back. Grab one of his ankles from behind and kick the back of the immobilized knee with the shin of the corresponding leg. Use the hips in a twisting and pushing forward motion in order to power this far relative of a 'Low Kick'. As he bends forward, catch him in the face or trunk with a Front Kick from behind. To finish him up, grab both ankles and pull them while you deliver a powerful Heel Front Kick to his tailbone. The coccyx is very sensitive and linked to both the hip joints and the spinal joints. On top of the serious damage from the Joint Kicks, the attacker will fall forward on his face.

➡️

*A sophisticated drill with two Joint Kicks; excellent for drilling situational kicking*

Our second special related technique is a *compounded Joint Attack* for use in close combat. It starts with a classic joint attack that is not a kick, but still extremely effective. Placing your foot behind his to lock it in place, you use your knee over his front lower leg to straighten it and push it down. This is a technique typical of East Asian and Chinese styles that immobilizes the opponent for further attacks or that can cause him to fall. When executed brusquely, it is a *near-Joint Kick* and can cause damage to the knee joint, and that is what we are striving for. But in this case, we shall compound the damage. As soon as he starts to 'give' to the Lock and loses his balance, you pull the leg back and away for some momentum. And then kick through his lower leg on the inside with a *Low Roundhouse Sweep Kick*. This maneuver is much easier than it seems and the fast double jolt on his joint is very damaging.

*Knee-locking attack followed fast by Low Roundhouse Sweep Kick*

Another technique *similar enough* to our Kick is presented below. You evade an opponent's Front Kick to the outside and strike with both hands on both sides of the knee in order to push the leg down. Keep your upper hand over his knee and push down while roundhouse-kicking his landing ankle. This causes a hyperextension of the knee and should also get him to the ground. Follow up.

*Hyperextend a landing leg with a hooking Roundhouse through the ankle*

**THE LOW ROUNDHOUSE TO THE BACK OF THE KNEE     57**

Simply kicking violently *through the standing leg of a kicker* is a joint attack per se. You can kick the ankle, the calf or the back of the knee, so long as you make sure to kick **through and with accelerating power**. This is also a mindset: do not attempt to sweep or push: kick to harm! Really striking a twisting leg carrying the full body weight will definitely hurt the knee joint.

*Cutting Kicks by Nimrod De Bremaeker: absorb the opponent's Roundhouse and kick the ankle, the calf or the knee of the standing leg*

Instead of attacking the back of the knee, your 'hooking' Low Roundhouse Kick can try to cause joint damage *to the inside ankle,* and at the same time cause the opponent to fall. This, again, is not a Sweep but a **kick-through joint attack**. The Figures below show how to plunge forward with a feinting Cross Punch that will become a grab. The lunge forward will help to power a strong Low Roundhouse. Push the opponent's shoulder down to help his fall and conclude by stomping his ankle for more damage.

*Lunge with a punching feint for a damaging 'hooking' Roundhouse to the inside ankle*

Another way to set up this variation is presented below, but it is suitable for the flexible fighters only: you pull the opponent's attention up with a high Front-leg Hopping Roundhouse Kick and attack his front ankle directly from the chamber-back position! Kick *through*, with some '*hooking in*'.

*Double no-touchdown Roundhouse Kick: high to the head and low to the front ankle*

Yet another way to use that variation is as a pure *Cutting Kick*. In the example illustrated below, you stop-punch a developing rear-leg Penetrating Front Kick and immediately kick the standing leg, before the kicking leg has even had the time to land. Such a kick to a standing leg (dynamically holding all the opponent's weight) is definitely not conducive to joint health.

*Cutting Kick: Hooking Roundhouse to the ankle of a standing leg*

**THE LOW ROUNDHOUSE TO THE BACK OF THE KNEE    59**

An even simpler *Cutting Kick* application is illustrated below; this time, against a high Roundhouse attack. You will simply attack directly the standing ankle with a powerful **Body-bent rear-leg 'hooking' Roundhouse**. The attacking leg will either be above your head level, or you will be able to absorb it in your shoulder or arm.

*Another joint-damaging Cutting Kick*

**It does not matter how slowly you go as long as you do not stop.**
**~Confucius**

# 6. The Front Leg Scissors

*Tesoura (Capoeira), Kani Basami (Judo)*

### General

This is a very common maneuver in many styles where ground-fighting is relevant. It was very typical to old *Ju-Jitsu*, from where it passed in a watered-down version into *Judo*, but from which it was subsequently banned because deemed too dangerous. The principle is very simple: you block the ankle with one leg, and you kick the front or side of the opponent's knee with the other foot. You cause both joint damage and a take-down. But the scissoring movement takes the basic mild principle a little bit further: you can do more than just block the ankle, you can in fact kick the opponent's foot/ankle simultaneously in the opposite direction (of the knee kick), so as to cause even more damage. This is the true **Joint Kick version**.

The basic technique can be executed in two ways: You attack the side of the knee either with a Hook Kick, or with a Roundhouse Kick; of course, the other leg blocks the ankle. Both ways are equally damaging to the joint, and both variations will be presented here. The set-up for this Kick can be achieved in many ways, from a standing, a sitting or a lying-down position; we provide examples and the reader is left to his own experience and imagination.

It should be note that the **Scissor Kick** is an excellent weapon to damage the elbow joint too, especially in groundfighting.

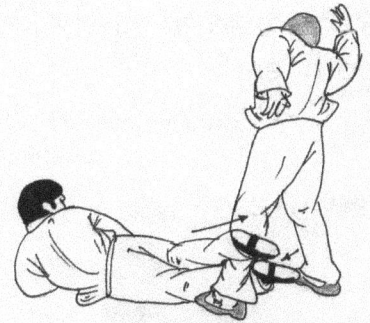

*You can scissor by attacking the knee (in this case sideways) with a Hook kick or with a Roundhouse Kick; the other foot scissors at the ankle*

*The Roundhouse version of the Ground Kick, to the front of the knee*

*Also great to attack the opponent's elbow joint on the ground*

## Description

The first Drawings show *the Ground Hook Kick version* against a standing opponent: Place one foot between his legs and hook from the inside behind his heel. Attack the side of his knee from the outside with a *Hook Kick*, rolling into the Kick with your whole body. Remember to scissor-kick with both feet!

*Ground Hook Kick to the knee with scissoring at the ankle*

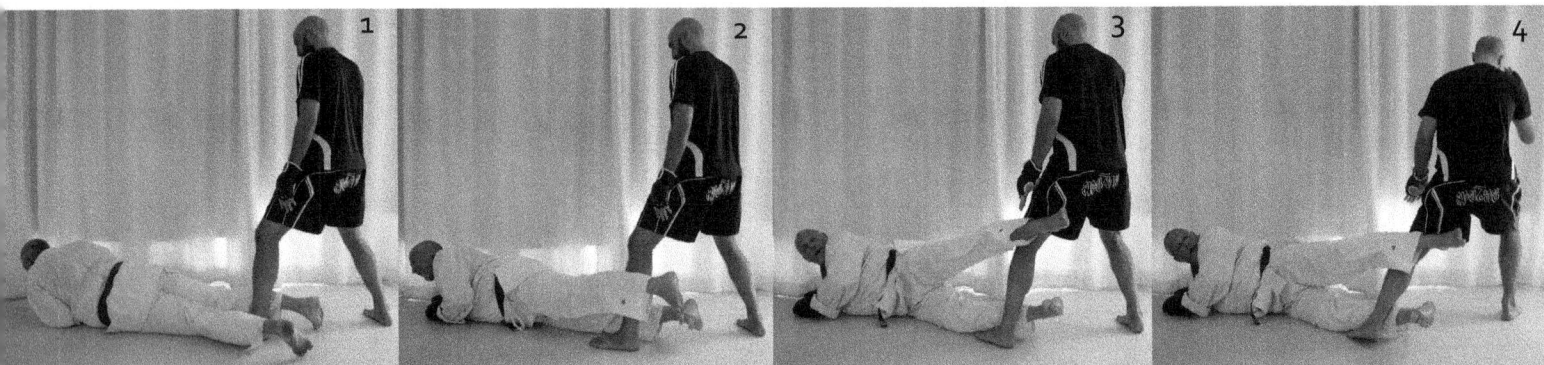

*Hook Kick to the **outside** knee*

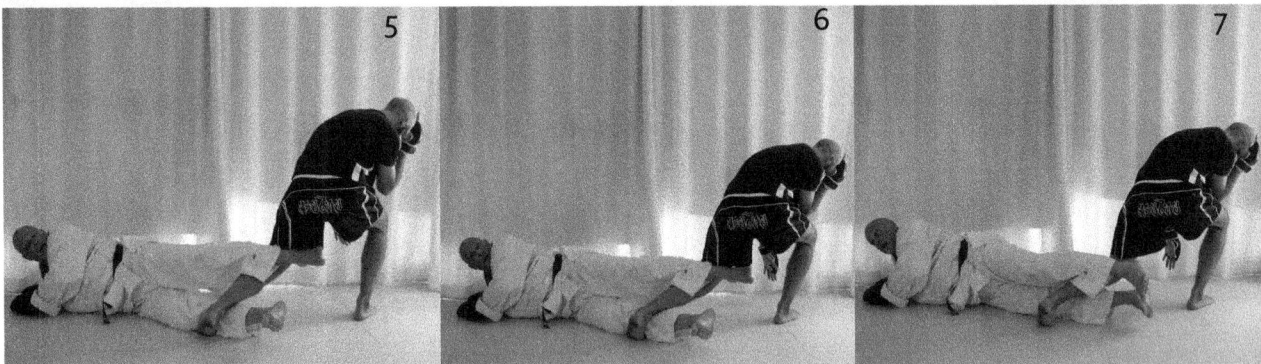

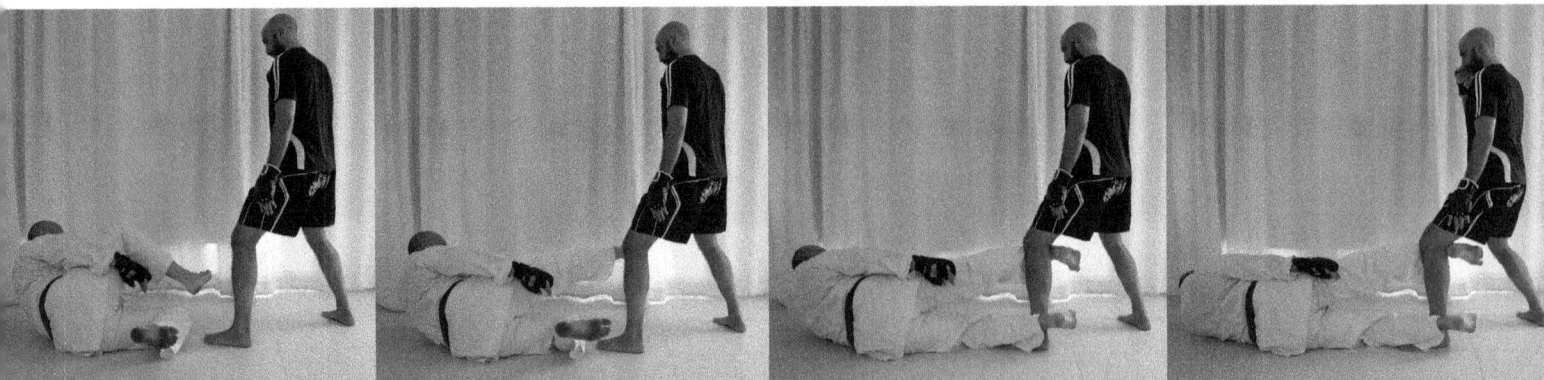

*Hook Kick to the **inside** knee*

The next Figures show the **Drop Roundhouse Kick version**, in a way very common to *Capoeira* practice: From a standing position, feint high and drop while placing both legs on each side of the opponent's front leg. Deliver a *Roundhouse Kick* to the inside of the front knee, while rolling violently with the whole body. Remember to scissor at the ankle and remember that it is not a takedown but a *Joint Kick*.

*A Sacrifice Kick: Drop Roundhouse the knee while scissoring at the ankle*

### Key Points

- This is a Kick to the joint first, and a Takedown only far second. *Concentrate on hurting the joint,* and he'll fall anyway.
- Always *use your whole body* for kicking, rolling powerfully into the move.

### Typical Application

The key to the success of the technique is the set-up. Once you are in "scissoring" position, the amount of effort needed is minimal and there is not much your opponent can do. Therefore, a lot of work is to be done *on the preparation and the entry*. The next Figures show a typical set-up against a high kicker: As your opponent starts a rear-leg high Roundhouse, you go down with a very deep forward cross-step which brings your formerly-rear leg behind his standing leg. Hook-kick violently his standing knee and follow up.

*The technique as a Drop Cutting Hook Kick, against a high Roundhouse*

## Specific Training

As mentioned, the key to success is *the set-up*. Drill all possible entries with a partner, no need for the full Kick execution each time. You can start by practicing all entries described in this section, then work on your personal favorites.

## Self defense

The next Drawings show the use of the *Hook Kick-version* against a standing opponent threatening you as you sit on the floor. Get smoothly into 'chambered' position and kick with both legs in opposite direction. Aim for the knee. Then flow into a natural Leg-lock and from this controlling position, hit his back and the back of his neck.

*Ground Hook Kick to checked knee, naturally followed by Leg Lock*

3                                            4                                            5

The coming Drawings, *at the top of next page*, show another set-up: You let yourself fall down backwards as your opponent lunges forward with a surprising straight knife attack. This evasion is reminiscent of the "*Drop Kicks*" already encountered in previous books. You smoothly and immediately straighten your legs on both sides of his front leg. Roundhouse-kick harshly the in-side of his knee while kicking his ankle in the other direction. It goes without saying that you must kick violently, target the knee precisely and use the whole body for maximum power. Follow up.

➡️

**1**

**2**

**3**

*When left no choice, evade by dropping to the ground and scissor-kick the assailant's front knee*

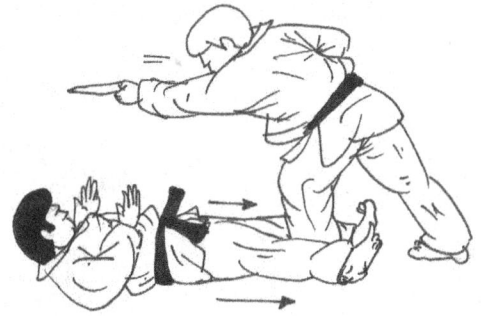

**4**

**5**

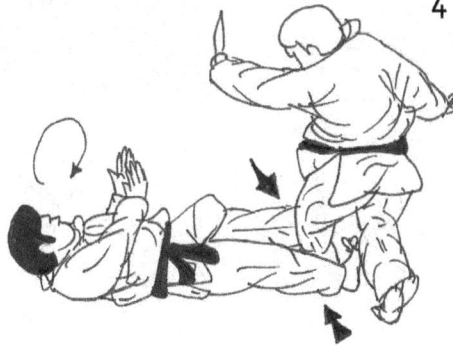

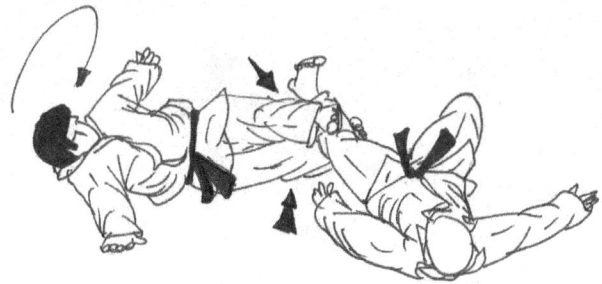

Our last Illustrations for this Chapter show an interesting but much more complex variation typical to Indonesian *Penchak Silat* styles. In a very typical 'Suicide' attack, you dive to catch both your opponent's wrists and then let yourself fall down on your back. You pull on the wrists while kicking upwards into his chin. Ouch! You then kick down on his arm with same kicking leg, and bend it over his elbow joint to then come encircling it (You keep hold of the wrists!). Do not let go of the wrist as you hook the inside of the knee, and then hook-kick with the other leg. Roll with your opponent and keep the painful Arm-lock with your leg and with all your body weight. The Drawings and some practice will make it very clear. Practice carefully in training though, as a violent kick & roll will dislocate his shoulder.

*Typical complex Indonesian maneuver where the Leg Scissor causes serious joint damage to the arm!"]*

To conclude, we illustrate in Photos the *Hook version* of the Kick from the ground, possibly after having been taken down by the opponent.

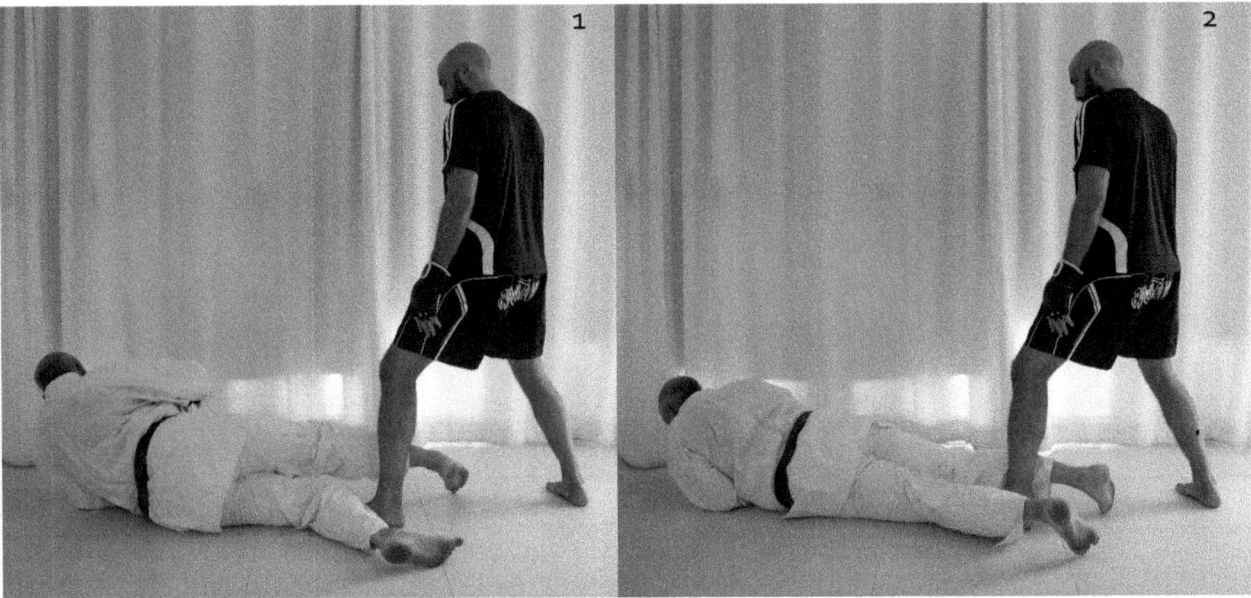

*Hook Kick version of the Kick; note the full roll*

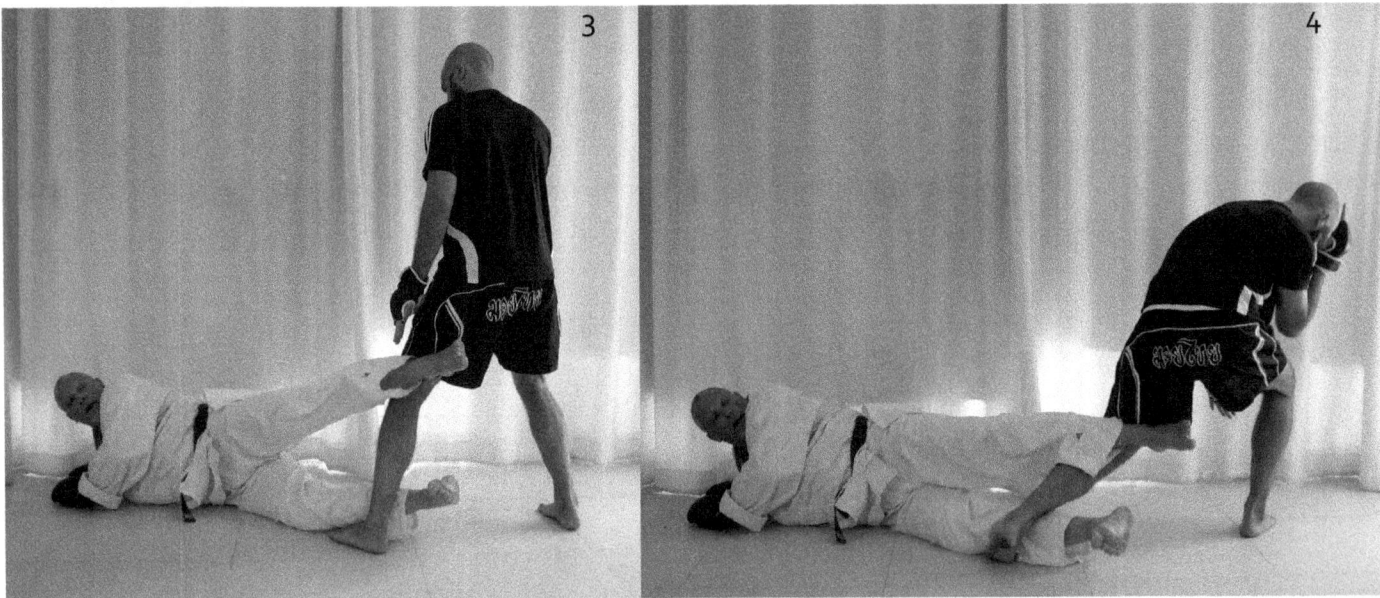

**Success isn't always about greatness. It's about consistency. Consistent hard work leads to success. Greatness will come. ~Dwayne Johnson**

# 7. THE TWO-LEGS SCISSOR KICK

*Tesoura (Capoeira), Kani Basami (Judo)*

### General

**The 2-legs Scissor Kick** is not very different from the one-leg version. In fact, in *Capoeira* and *Ju-Jitsu*, these kicks bear the same name: in the heat of battle you scissor what is in the way of your legs as per your set-up, whether it is one leg or two legs.

The original *Kani Basami* of old *Ju-Jitsu* was a Joint Kick aiming for the front of the knees. With the transition to *Judo*, the maneuver became a take-down and the scissoring was done higher on the thigh to avoid joint damage. Even this throw was later judged too dangerous and its use forbidden in *Randori* and in sport *Judo*, to be finally fully dropped from the curriculum.

The old *Ju-jitsu* Throw is presented in the coming illustrations, and its use in an offensive combination is illustrated in the Photos.

*The Kani Basami Takedown – forbidden in Judo*

*Roundhouse, Backfist, Hook Kick, Kani Basami, Ground Axe Kick*

## Description

Just like for the one-leg version, the Kick can be delivered either as a Roundhouse Kick or as a Hook Kick *__to the front of the knees__*. The other leg scissors at the ankles and the whole body is used to power the Kick.

The first set of Illustrations shows the set up and delivery of **the Hook Kick version**.

Note the full body twist during the kick.

*The Hook Kick version of the 2-legs Scissor kick*

3

4

5

1

2

The next set of Drawings illustrates the same for **a Roundhouse Kick version**. This is not a Takedown, but a Double Kick!

*A Roundhouse version of the 2-legs Scissor kick, with a full twist*

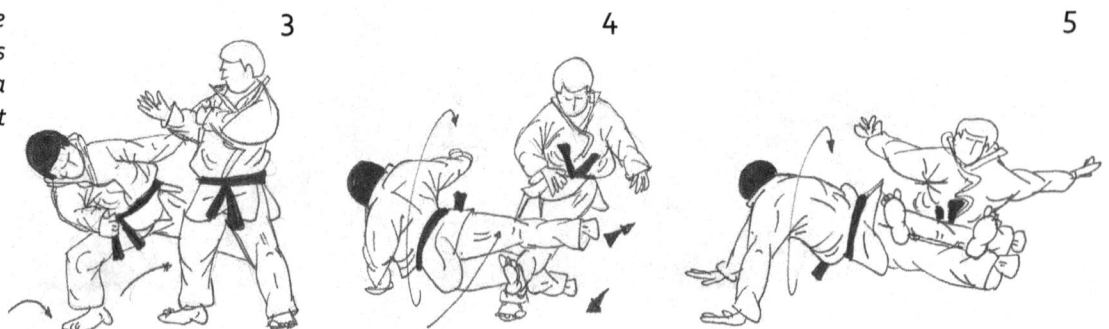

3

4

5

## Key Points

- *Use the whole body as you kick*, twisting into the kick for maximum power.
- Aim *precisely at the front of the knee* for lock and for maximum joint damage.
- Kick the back of the ankles *in the opposite direction*.

## Specific Training

- Practice the set-up (entry), the explosiveness and the power of the Kick *on a heavy bag marked at knee level* and hold up by a partner (See Figure).
- Practice the *kick-through* on a body shield held by a partner (See second Figure).

*Drill on a heavy bag*

*Also drill on the body shield for kick-through*

## Self defense

The following set of Drawings shows the technique as the follow-up of a fast front-leg Hand-on-floor high Hook Kick. You first get his attention down with a hand feint towards his testicles, and hop immediately into a high Hand-on-floor Hook Kick that will keep your head out of reach of a possible counter. Your kicking leg comes down directly into position for a second Hook kick through the knees. Of course, your other leg scissor-kicks his ankles. Follow up on the ground.

*Hook kick version of the 2-legs Scissor Kick, after a first high Hook Kick*

# 8. THE FRONT LEG OUTSIDE HOOK

*Tesoura de Frente (Capoeira)*

## General

This is a very specific *Capoeira* maneuver, although some similar techniques are found in *Silat* styles. One could argue that it is not really a Kick, but it is a very interesting move and therefore described for the sake of completeness. We will present it as such, the way it is practiced, as an application with no more discussion.

## Description and Application

The Drawings show how you crowd your opponent and hook your rear leg behind his front leg from the outside. In the same uninterrupted movement, you let yourself fall on his hip, while lifting his front ankle up. The **Joint Attack** is basically executed with your hip/pelvis on his upper front knee while you lift his ankle with the leg. The advantage of the technique is that you let yourself fall with your whole weight on his upper leg. If you do this in a controlled way, it is a good take-down. But if you kick up vigorously to lift his leg while hitting his upper thigh with your pelvis, it is a very serious joint attack. Follow up on the ground.

*Hook his front leg from the outside and entangle his ankle, then kick up while letting you fall down on his front thigh*

This technique will remind old-school *Judokas* like myself of the now-forbidden '*Tagaku Gake*' technique. This 'Leg Entanglement Takedown' has been banned from competitive *Judo*, and is known very seldom taught, even in *traditional* Judo. For reference we show one of its version, (starting as an *O Uchi Gari*), in the Illustrations below. It is a fantastic technique!

*Old Judo's* **Tagaku Gake**: *similar in principle and banned because dangerous to the opponent's joint*

**If you always put limit on everything you do, physical or anything else. It will spread into your work and into your life. There are no limits. There are only plateaus, and you must not stay there, you must go beyond them.**
**~Bruce Lee**

# 9. THE GROUND SIDE KICK TO CHECKED KNEE

*Hiza Basami (Shorinji-ryu Kenkokan), Deng Tui (Kung Fu)*

### General

This is a very classic Kick in ground and eclectic self-defense styles, as it is extremely effective. You check your opponent's ankle from behind, and you side-kick the front of his knee. For the joint, it does not get worse than that. Of course, you can side-kick the inside or the outside of the knee joint with the same results of joint damage; it will depend on the circumstances and on the reaction of the opponent.

The technique is easy to execute by itself, but it is the set-up that will ensure success. This Kick is a must-practice, and a very important tool if you find yourself on the ground. Well-executed, it can simply win you the fight.

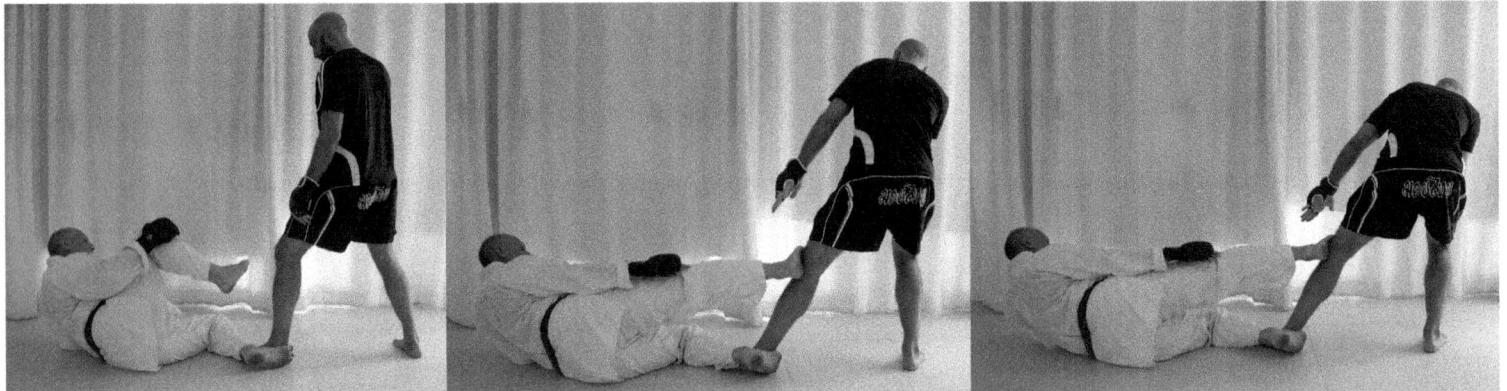

*The Side Kick to the front of the checked knee*

*The Side Kick to the inside of the checked knee*

## Description

The Illustrations show the execution of the Kick after a typical *Kung Fu* entry. Practice this technique slowly at the beginning, then accelerate as you master the form. Let yourself fall down on the floor as a large cross-step gets your formerly rear foot behind his front ankle, from his in-side. This should be delivered as one smooth uninterrupted move. Hook behind his front ankle and pull forward as you side-kick forcefully the front of his knee joint. It looks easy but requires lots of practice; it then becomes very effective.

*The Ground Side Kick to Checked Knee, Kung-fu style*

The coming Illustrations show the **opposite way of entry** for the same technique (*Opposite Guards*); and this time, as your opponent jabs.Here is our example: *In opposite stances*, you evade a Jab by kneeling down, and then by rolling back on the floor as your front leg glides to hook his front ankle from the in-side. Roll to the side as you side-kick the front of his knee with your rear leg. Note that, if the opponent moves and twists his leg, the technique stays as effective: you side-kick the side of his knee instead of the front of his knee. In any case, you should keep ground-kicking after that to finish the fight.

*Entry for the technique in opposite stances*

3

4

5

## Key Points

- Pull the *ankle* forward violently as you kick the knee!
- Kick *through* the knee, do not push. Pushing the knee results in a take-down, you want joint damage.
- Push with the *hips* into the Kick.

## Specific Training

- The key to success is the *entry*: Train the setting up of the technique on a standing bag, repetitively without executing the whole kick. Work on all set-ups described in this section. Get familiar, and then work for the speed of the set-up (See Figure).
- Drill the entry and the smooth hooking of the ankle with a *partner*.

## Typical Application

The coming Figures show the classic use of the technique as a Ground Kick: You are lying on your back and your opponent is standing in front of you. If your legs are not between his, get them there and proceed fast before he takes advantage of his high ground. Roll on your side while hooking the ankle and chamber the other leg. Kick *through* the knee and follow up.

*The classic Ground Side kick to checked knee*

3

4

5

## Self defense

The coming Illustrations show a very useful application of the technique against an attempted Wrist-lock. In this case, your assailant has got you in a side wrist-lock (very typical of the *Hakko-ryu Jju Jitsu* style) and presses you down. Instead of resisting, you let yourself fall down brusquely and hook his rear ankle (as you are close) with your rear leg. Kick the knee while pulling the ankle, and follow up.

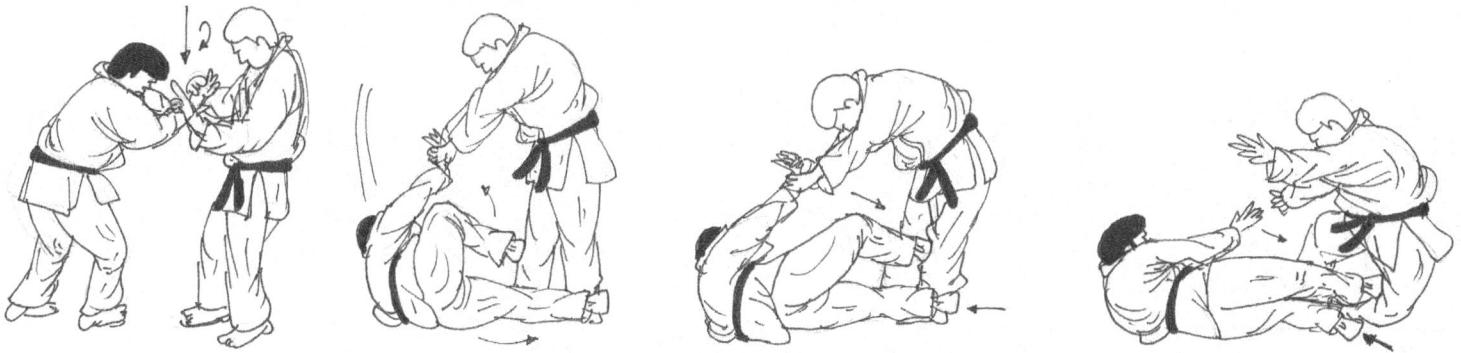

*Instead of resisting a Wrist Lock, dive down into the joint Kick*

The next set of Drawings shows the application of the kick as a **Drop Kick** against a high kicking attack. In this application, it can sometimes be difficult to hit the front of the knee, but the side will do as well. Should you have to kick the back of the knee, it still results in a nasty fall and some knee damage, although much less severe. Against a front-leg high Hook Kick (or Side Kick), bend your legs to significantly lower your stance, as you control the kick from below. Let yourself fall to the ground as your rear foot comes to hook the standing ankle of the attacker. Kick *through* the knee! Then follow up.

*Drop kick against a high kicker*

3

4

5

The last Figures show a knife defense application. Against a full-step lunging straight knife attack, you let yourself fall down on the side in a *Drop Side Kick* to the exposed ribs. The Drop Kick is both a Stop Kick and an evasion from the knife strike. Hook behind his ankle from the out-side and deliver a second Side Kick, this time to the front of his knee. Kick *through* the knee with the mindset of breaking it. Stand up fast as he falls down and try to attack his exposed groin. Remember to control the knife hand as you follow up, with a strike towards the eyes for example.

1    2    3    4

5

*Committed knife poke:*
*Drop Side Stop Kick*
*followed by Ground Side*
*Kick to Checked Knee*

6    7

8    9

## It is not because things are difficult that we do not dare, it is because we do not dare that they are difficult.
## ~Lucius Annaeus Seneca

# 10. THE GROUND SIDE KICK TO CHECKED ANKLE

*Alavanca de pé (Capoeira)*

## General

This is more of an anecdotal kick: It is the same Kick than the previous one, but instead of kicking the knee, you kick the shin just above the foot in order to hurt the ankle. As this Kick exists as a separate kick in *Capoeira* and in some Korean arts, we present here for the sake of completeness.

## Description

You hook behind your opponent's foot and kick his shin just above the ankle. As illustrated, you can kick with the blade of the foot or with the whole plant of the foot.

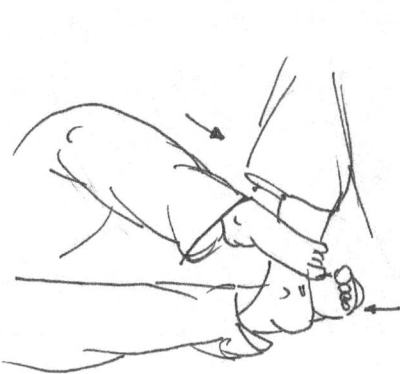

*Hook the foot from behind and kick just above the ankle with blade of the foot...*

*...or with the whole plant of the foot*

## Key Points

- Kick *through* the shin.
- Do not push, *kick!*
- *Pull simultaneously* with the "hooking" foot.

## Typical Application

In theory, the Kick is applicable in all situations the previous Kick was relevant. As an illustration, we present here a very interesting example. Your opponent has succeeded to place you in a classic armlock position (*Hara Gatame – Judo*). Instead of resisting, throw yourself suddenly in Forward Roll (*Mae Ukemi*). As you land on your back, take hold of his wrist and pull him towards you to keep him busy and to prevent him from getting away. Place the Kick and follow up.

*Use the Kick after a somersault to escape an armlock*

# 11. THE DOWNWARD KICK TO KICKING-KNEE JOINT

## General

This is a very effective and sophisticated technique, somewhere between a Leg-lock, a Take-down and a Joint Kick. The more power and speed you put into the movement, the more of a Kick it is, and the more dangerous it is for the joint. Practice carefully.
As it is a very specific kick against 'caught legs', we shall therefore directly present applications.

## Typical Applications

The first set of Drawings shows how you control a high Roundhouse with a rear-hand block, and then deliver a *Downward Heel Kick* <u>from as high as possible</u> to the immobilized knee joint. This 'Axe' Kick climbs up as an Inside Crescent. Be very careful in practice, this is a very dangerous technique for the knee joint.

*The dangerous Joint Kick against a checked high Roundhouse Kick*

The next Drawings, *at the top of next page*, illustrate a more complex variation, against a scooped Side Kick. Deliver the *Downward Heel (Axe) Kick* to the immobilized knee, but aiming to finish it in a Side Kick Chamber position. After kicking *through* the joint, you start bending the leg to achieve the chamber. Release the caught foot as you side-kick the knee of his standing leg.

➡

*Axe Kick to the opponent's caught leg, turning into a Cutting Side Kick*

The coming Figures show a variation of the Kick **turning into a very mean Leg-lock.**
Evade back the opponent's front-leg Side Kick just enough to catch his foot. Deliver the
*Axe Kick*, but this time with some more circular action: You both twist the foot slightly
and you round the Kick around the knee as you kick down. Lower the kicking foot down
while accentuating the torque of the lock and sit on the locked leg. Finish by grabbing
his collar to punch the back of his head, repeatedly if necessary.

1           2

*Axe Kick to Leg Lock*

3           4           5           6

The next Illustrations show a variation of the Kick in an application *about scooping a kicking leg*. The variation is especially interesting **for fighters with less flexibility** who would struggle to lift the kicking leg very high for momentum. In our example, you catch the kicking leg and strike the side of his knee with your hand and/or forearm. The purpose of the strike is both to make the leg turn and to cause joint damage; hit hard and through. Then push down to take him to the ground. Keep his ankle high and under control, and then kick down *through* the knee of the immobilized leg. After impact, bend your kicking leg in Leg Lock set up and sit down. Push his foot down towards his buttock; your leg behind his knee joint will cause a very dangerous and painful hyperextension Lock.

*Against a kick: a variation of the Axe Kick leading to a hard Leg Lock*

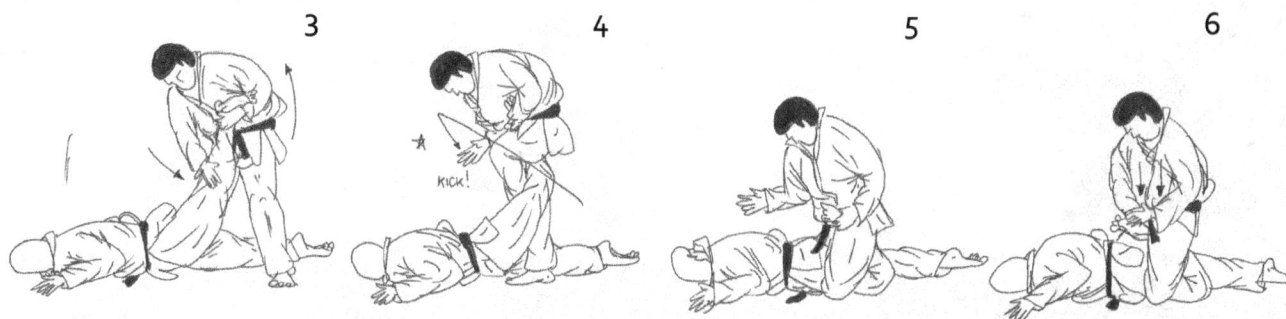

The following example is also for **less flexible Artists** and is closely related to the previous technique. This is more of a *Hybrid Kick* than a variation of the Downward Kick to the knee joint: there is a little bit of Inside Crescent and Roundhouse Shin. You block and scoop the kicking foot of your attacker, and strike his side knee with a Hammer-fist or Forearm Strike. Strike hard to hurt the joint, to make him pivot and to take him down. As soon as his knee is at the right height for you kick it over and down by going through a Roundhouse Chamber move. After impact, extend the leg while sitting on his knee. Leave one leg into the back of his knee joint and push his ankle towards his buttocks for a painful Leg Lock.

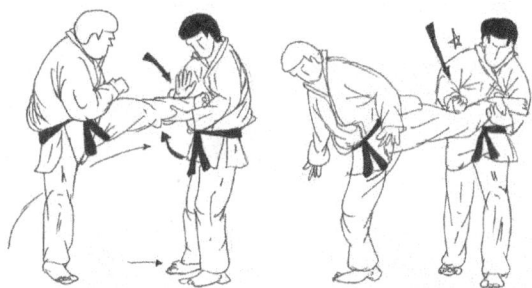

*Against a Kick: scoop and attack the knee joint with a Roundhouse Chamber version of a Downward Kick*

# 12.  THE SPIN-BACK SCISSOR KICK

## General

This is a close relative of the Drop Spin-back Hook Kick and of the Downward Drop Spin-back Hook Kick presented in our 'Essential Book of Martial Arts Kicks'. The difference is only the **emphasis on the joint attack**. The Kick is simply a drop spin-back hook kick aiming at one or two <u>knees</u>. Because it is delivered close to the opponent, you usually strike his knee with your calf and not with the foot. Remember though: This is a **Kick,** and not a pushy Take-down.

*Applied Essential Drop Spin-back Hook Kick*

*Another applied Drop Spin-back Hook Kick*

## Description

The coming Illustrations, *at the top of next page*, show the **classic** set-up and execution as a single-leg attack: Slide your front foot besides and behind your opponent's front foot (on his out-side). In a smooth move, drop on your front knee while starting the Spin-back and the Hook Kick. Aim for the *knee* of his front leg, immobilized by your own foot.

➡️

*The classic Spin-back Scissor Kick to one leg*

## Key Points

- Kick *through*, no pushing.
- Use the whole *twisting motion of the body* to put power into the Kick
- Always *follow up*.
- The step, drop, twist and kick are one smooth and *uninterrupted* movement.

## Typical Application

The coming Drawings show a typical setup for the Kick: You deliver a mid-level (preferably groin) front-leg Hopping Roundhouse, then chamber back and lower the leg directly outside his front foot. Keeping the circular momentum, you drop and deliver the **Spin-back Scissor**. This time try to hit *through* his back knee with your heel, while your calf will take care of the immobilized front knee. *Think of joint damage!* Follow up with one or more Downward Heel Kicks.

*A good combo: Groin Roundhouse to Drop Spin-back Scissor kick to the knees*

### Specific Training

- Drill the *set-up to Drop move* on the heavy bag.
- Practice with a *partner*.

### Self defense

The next set of Illustrations shows a simple execution, but this time you'll cause the assailant to fall *on his face*. In opposite stances, you evade your opponent's Reverse Punch (Cross) by spinning back while dropping down on your front knee. Kick to scissor his front knee and follow up.

*Scissor Kick to the front knee in opposite stances*

The last example shows the technique used against a *Low Kick* attack. You bend the leg, twist and drop to your knee in order to smother the Low Kick's impact: '*Go with the Kick*' maneuver. From that position spin-back and scissor both legs. Then, you can follow up with a Downward Roundhouse.

*The Kick as a natural counter to a classic Low Kick attack of your front knee*

3    4    5

# 13. THE UPWARD FRONT KICK TO THE ARM JOINTS

## General

This is a very simple Kick, of course: the basic Upward Front Kick, as described in the *'Essential Book of Martial Arts Kicks'*. But it is especially targeted at the upper limbs joints, generally the elbow, but also the wrist and the armpit. The emphasis will be here on the setting-up of the technique and the specificity of the target. We shall present several examples, in which you can hold the opponent's arm while kicking, or you can let go at impact. Both hurt the joint, though keeping the arm in place while kicking will do more damage. Obviously.

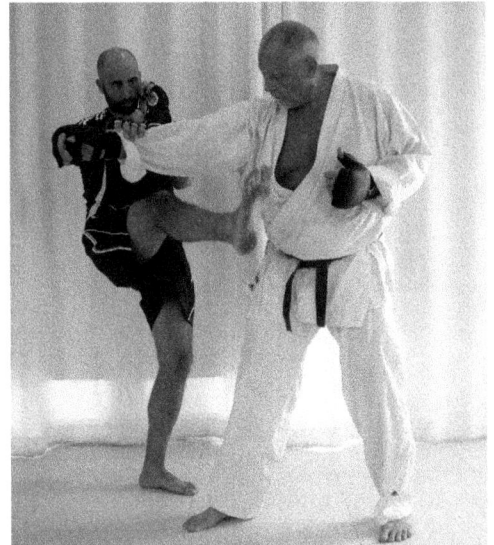

*Easy to understand: Kick through the elbow of the caught extended arm*

## Description

The coming Drawings show the classic delivery of the Kick: You evade forward and outwards when attacked by a full-step Lunge Punch, and you deliver the **Upward Front Kick** directly from the original rear leg position. Target the elbow and kick *through*. You can either let your opponent's arm go, or you can keep hold while kicking for even more damage. In the example we execute both: the first Kick attacks the elbow of the arm kept extended and in place by your hold; let the foot rebound on the ground for a second Upward Kick to the same elbow that you now let go of.

*Evade a punch forward and out, catch the arm and double-kick the elbow*

Kick the caught elbow twice; let go the second time

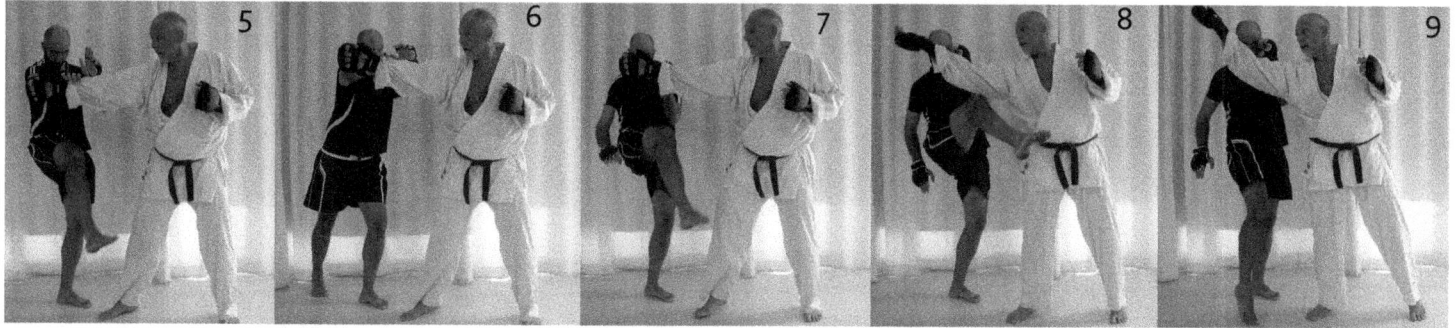

The next Drawing shows another classic: **the Upward Front Stop Kick to the armpit** of an attacking arm.

The orthodox techniques to be drilled are presented in the following sets of Photos; the first presents the more powerful rear-leg Kick, and the second illustrates the classic front-leg Kick.

Stop Kick to the armpit: kick hard and into the target

The classic rear-leg Upward Kick to the armpit

The classic front-leg Upward kick to the armpit

**THE UPWARD FRONT KICK TO THE ARM JOINTS**    87

## Key Points

- Kick fast, *precisely* and through. Power is less important.
- If you keep hold of the arm, *try to turn it upwards*, in such a way that you'll hit the elbow and not the side.

## Typical Application

The coming Figures show a simple and classic application against a downward strike with a baseball bat. The good thing with this type of attack is that the opponent will need to lift the bat up before attacking. Evade forward and out as the bat comes down. Control his hands and kick up *into* the elbows. Follow up.

*Evade a bat strike forward and out and kick up into the elbows*

## Specific Training

Drill the classic Upward Front Kick for *speed and flexibility*, as described in previous work. Drill with a partner holding a focus pad or a body shield.

*Drill the Upward Front Kick, for example against a body shield*

## Self defense

Most self-defense applications of this specific Kick are against knife attacks. Although very difficult and dangerous to execute in real life, they are interesting to *drill* for the experienced Martial Artist.[*Refer to our books about Krav Maga*]
The first set of Drawings shows how you retreat against a straight knife thrust and stop-kick the assailant with a ***front-leg Upward Front Kick*** to the armpit. Follow up, of course. This is best used against an assailant toying with you with threatening pokes.

*Half-a-step or a full step back to get out of range of a knife poke; front-leg Front Kick to the exposed armpit*

The next set of Drawings shows that, if you have retreated too much to his attack, you can still kick the elbow or the wrist from where you are. Follow up, of course. (*Not recommended in a real life situation!*)

*If you have evaded too far, you can still kick the elbow or wrist, and then follow up with aggressive kicking*

The set of Illustrations *coming at the top of next page* shows how you evade out the same poking attack, but, this time, you forcefully block down the attacking wrist and grab it. You keep hold of the arm as you kick the elbow, for maximum damage. You then lower the leg deep behind him and use the other leg for a Stomp Kick to the back of his knee. Simultaneously, you claw his eyes from behind to pull his head back. Finish with a downward elbow strike to the face. (*That's more like it!*)

➤

*Evade out on the knife poke, grab the wrist and kick up the elbow. Follow up*

And the coming set of Photos, in turn, will show the Kick used as a *Stop Kick* against a simple Jab: a ***front-leg Upward Front Stop Kick*** to the exposed armpit will stop him in his tracks. Kick *through* the shoulder joint with the mindset of causing damage!

*Stop Kick to the opponent's armpit exposed by his jabbing*

The coming Illustrations will show a very simple and natural version of the Kick, but in a more sophisticated application. What you should take away from this exercise, is that, *if you hold the wrist of a downed opponent, it is easy and advised to front-kick his extended elbow*. In the example, you block a very wide Swing Punch (*Haywire Punch*) and catch the back of the neck of the attacker for a body-twisting Takedown. As soon as he lands on his back before you, kick his extended elbow with your shin. Kick _through and hard_, and follow up.

*Body-twisting Takedown followed by a vicious Shin Kick to the extended elbow of the downed opponent*

The next Application will present the Front Kick directed at the hip or at the higher thigh area of an opponent, in order to cause pain and mollify him for a Takedown. The intended Throw is Judo's *Uki Otoshi*, a very simple twisting off-balancing technique. Kicking up his hip while setting him up (*Kuzushi*) will help the Takedown and cause him some hip joint damage at the same time. A Joint Front Kick, though not to upper limbs!

*Front Upward Kick to the hip to help an Uki Otoshi Takedown*

The next example, *illustrated at the top of next page*, is also a '**Destruction series**', but starting from the classic *Upward Front Kick to the elbow of a Punching arm*. It is the lowering of the leg that will strive to add as much joint damage as possible. After the Timing Stop Kick, the kicking leg will directly go to *stomp* the befuddled opponent's front knee. From there, it can glide on the shin to come and *stomp* the ankle and upper foot with your body weight. Keep your stomping foot in place and use your other foot for a Front Kick to the side of his rear *knee*. ➡

*Joint attack series after an Upward Front Stop Kick to the elbow*

# 14. THE UPWARD SIDE KICK TO THE ARM JOINTS

## General

This is of course the side version of the previous Kick. It is a simple **Upward Side Kick** as presented in our book about '*Essential Kicks*'. But this is a Kick that you will deliver to the wrist, to the elbow or to the armpit of your opponent. Again, you can either hold his arm in place while you kick the joint, or kick the joint of the free arm.

*Upward Side Kick to the armpit of the free arm developing a Jab*

*Upward Side kick to the armpit of a 'caught' arm*

## Description

The Drawing shows the execution of the Kick to the elbow, while holding your opponent's arm. In fact, it shows the ideal position, in which you rotate his wrist to have his elbow pointing downwards in the path of the Kick. But the Applications will also present variations in which the opponent's arm is free.

*Side Kick to immobilized elbow*

### Key Points

- Again, like with the Front Kick: kick *fast and through*. No need for power.
- If you control your opponent's arm, *twist it* (elbow towards the kick) and extend it if possible, for maximum damage.

### Typical Applications

The coming Figures illustrate a classic application against a "Front kick/Jab" kind of opponent. As your opponent attacks with a rear-leg Penetrating Front Kick, you retreat half-a-step. As he lands and delivers his Jab, you use your formerly rear leg to deliver an **Upward Side Kick** to his incoming elbow. Follow up, of course.

*Half-a-step retreat and Upward Side Kick to incoming elbow*

The next set of Illustrations shows a classic **offensive** combination in which <u>you open your opponent's guard by kicking up his front elbow</u> as he is in guard. This works especially well on adversaries who flourishingly hold their hands away from their bodies. You then chamber back and immediately switch to a Penetrating Side Kick to his now exposed ribs (without lowering the foot back to the ground). It is generally necessary to hop a little for the second Kick. Also a great exercise to drill for overall kicking proficiency.

*Use the Upward Side kick to lift the opponent's guard and follow up*

## Specific Training

Refer to the relevant section of 'The Essential Book of Martial Arts Kicks'.

- Train your *flexibility* for kicking speed
- Drill the Upward Side Kick *on a focus pas held by a partner* at shoulder level. Make sure you kick *through*!

## Self defense

The Figures below show, again, a self-defense application against an incoming stepped Knife Stab. Evade the stab by pivoting back and down, fast. Place your hands on the floor while you are kicking his incoming *armpit* from this position. Kick *through* the joint. Follow up immediately with a flurry of Body-bent Kicks to the groin and the knees.

*Spin-down evasion to a hand-on-floor position; stop-kick the stabbing armpit from below*

We shall conclude with a ***traditional*** exercise. You will block a classic Stepping Punch to the head with an Upward Block (*Age Uke – Karatedo*). Pull back your front foot to adjust the distance and execute a fast *front-leg Upward Side Kick* to his upper arm. Kick *through* the arm to cause joint damage. Lower the kicking foot deep forward with an Elbow Strike to the ribs, potentially exposed by the lifted arm.

*Upward Side kick towards the armpit after an Upward Block of a punching attack*

# 15. THE OUTSIDE CRESCENT KICK TO THE ELBOW

## General

**The Outside Crescent Kick** is a classic Joint Kick. Already when we presented this basic kick in our book about basic Essential Kicks its joint-attacking potential was emphasized. The Kick can be delivered on both sides of the elbow, and whether the arm is controlled or not. Examples of all variations will be provided. This is a must-practice Kick.

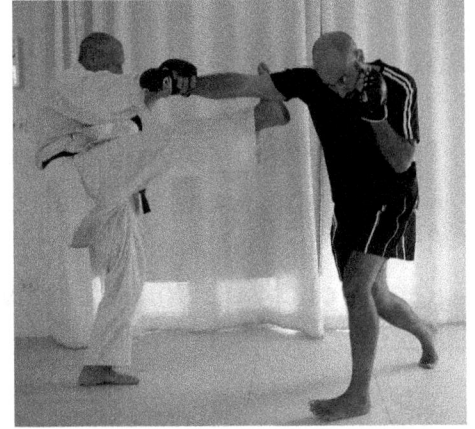

*The Outside Crescent Kick to an immobilized elbow*

*The Outside Crescent Kick against a free elbow*

*Kick through with power and the results are clearly visible*

## Description

The Drawings show the classic full joint attack with the Kick: You feint a high jab to force your opponent to block, and you catch the blocking wrist. Pull the arm to extend it and kick the elbow from the outside with your front leg, hopping if necessary. Kick fast and *through* the elbow. Pull the arm to extend it and try to twist it slightly to present the elbow to the coming Kick.

*The full joint attack: keep hold of the arm while you kick*

## Typical Applications

The Figures show the classic **'Guard Opener'** in which you attack **the inside** of the opponent's elbow, *without holding the arm*. This is still very painful and damaging to the joint. Here, your rear-leg Outside Crescent Kick has opened his guard and you land to his outside. Follow up with a rear-leg high Roundhouse, while his attention is focused on his painful and displaced arm.

*Kick the guard open with full power and follow up seamlessly*

And the next Photos, *at the top of next page*, illustrate the Kick **with the arm held in place**: Evade and catch a Cross Punch and kick the elbow. Follow up.

➡️

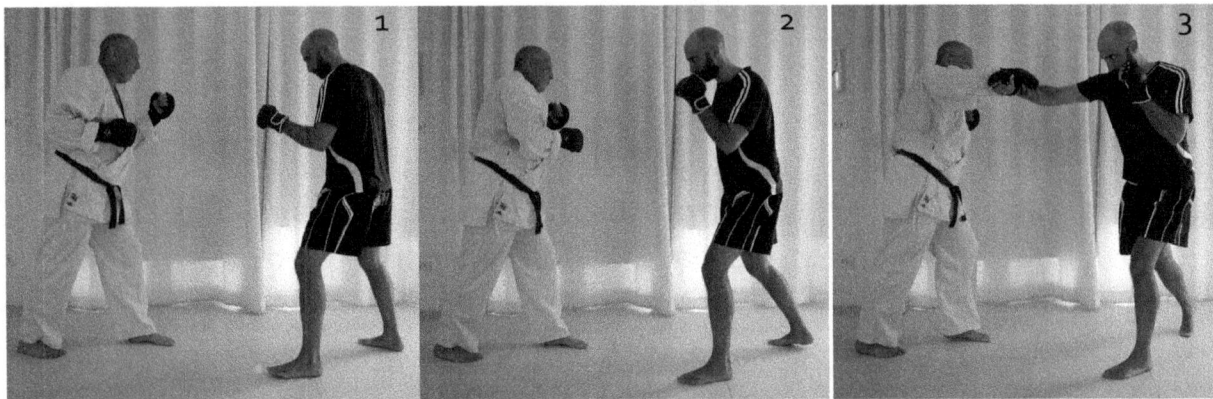

The full Joint attack against a Cross punch

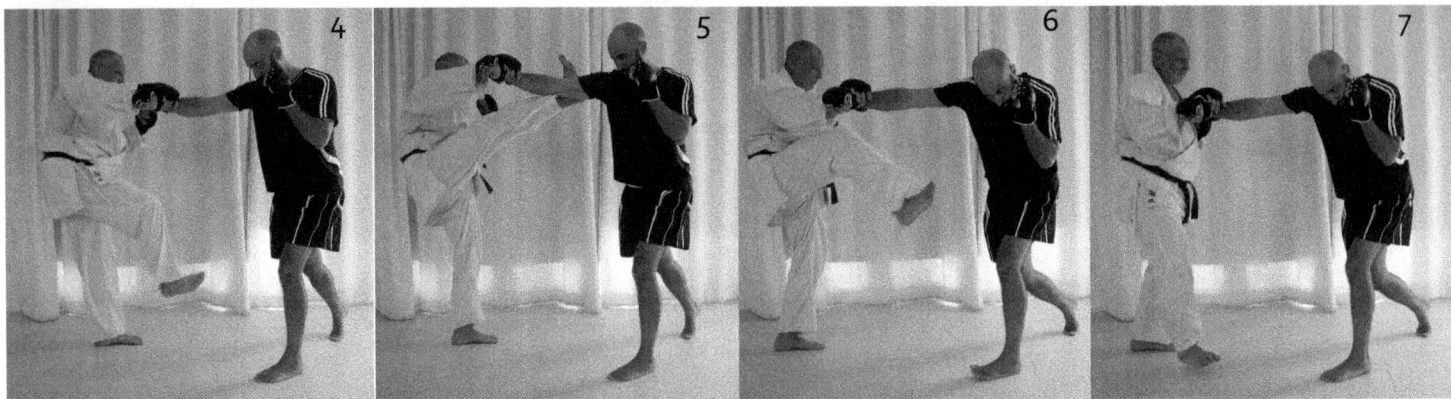

## Specific Training

- Drill the basic Outside Crescent Kick for *kick-through power.*
- Work on your *flexibility*.

*Drill the Kick on focus pads held by a partner*

## Self defense

The first Drawings, *at the top of next page*, show the use of the Kick *against a full-step Lunge Punch*: you evade forward and out, while getting hold of his attacking wrist. Deliver your **rear-leg Outside Crescent Kick to the controlled elbow,** and pivot directly into Side-kick Chamber without lowering the leg or releasing the wrist. Side kick the open ribs and follow up, for example, with a Stomping Side Kick to the back of his knee.

1    2    3    4

*Evade and catch a lunging Punch, kick the elbow and follow up with Side Kicks*

5    6    7

The next Illustrations describe an important use of the Kick **as a follow up to a take-down** in which you have control of one of your assailant's arms. In many *Judo* and *Ju-jitsu* throws, you keep control of your opponent's arms. But we shall describe here a more unorthodox 'Wrist Throw' from *Aiki-jitsu*. The assailant steps towards you and grabs your lapel. You do not resist but go with his momentum while catching his grabbing wrist. Twist and pull down your off-balanced opponent. As your opponent lands on his back, you pull on his arm to extend it and rotate it so as to have the elbow in the path of your **short Outside Crescent Kick**. Kick hard and *through*. Follow up with a head Stomp and a violent arm break (pulling the wrist out while immobilizing his elbow with your leg).

*Kick the extended elbow of an opponent you have just thrown to the ground*

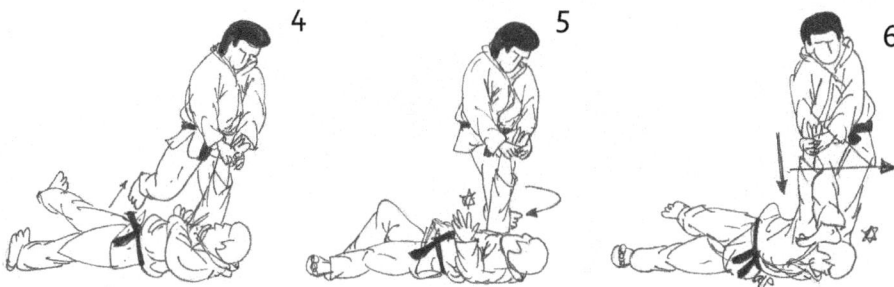

4    5    6

The Photos illustrate a simple follow-up after a **front-leg Outside Crescent to the opponent's guard**: a naturally-flowing Ridge-hand Strike.

*Front-leg Outside Crescent to guarding elbow and Ridge-hand follow-up*

The coming Illustrations shows the **Ground Kick variation**. As you lie on the floor, your assailant attempts to punch you. Roll on your side to block and catch his punch from his out-side. Pull his arm and kick the elbow. Keep pulling on his arm while Downward-heel kicking it. Simultaneously sweep his front foot from the inside with your other foot. Keep control of his arm while chambering for a harsh Heel Ground Front Kick to the face. Keep at it!

*The Ground version of the Outside Crescent to the elbow, and hard follow-ups*

3          4          5          6

The coming Drawings will illustrate an **offensive** use of the technique. You feint-jab in order to have him block: you can now grab his wrist while you put him off-balance with an Inside sweep of his front foot. Pull on his arm and use the same leg to kick his elbow from the outside (while keeping hold of it). Follow up.

*Offensive Sweep to Outside Crescent arm break*

We shall follow with an *interesting variation of the Outside Crescent*, not to the elbow, **but to the back of the opponent's knee** in certain very specific situations. You are lying on the ground and the attacker standing in front of you attempts a high-chambered Stomp Kick. Block and deviate the kick with an **Outside Crescent Ground Kick**. Keep your kicking block going until and after his foot lands on the floor; do not decelerate after impact. This way, you are in fact kicking the back of his knee with the whole energy of your wide trajectory.

*Very special: Outside Crescent Block & Joint Kick to the back of the knee*

And to conclude: another variation on the same theme is the **'short' Outside Crescent to the knee of a developing kick**. This technique looks like a simple Leg Block but is surprisingly damaging when well-timed. It is using the *shin* to connect. Kick *through* the target, and follow up, preferably with more attacks towards the same knee.

*Simple Outside Shin Crescent targeting the knee of a developing Front Kick with precision*

# There is no substitute for hard work.
# ~Thomas A. Edison

# 16. The Inside Crescent Kick to the Elbow and Apparented Techniques

## General

Again, the reader is invited to refer to our book about *Essential Kicks* where the basic **Crescent Kick** is described with already an emphasis on the joint attack aspect. The Kick is suitable to attack both sides of elbow, whether you hold it place or not.
The Kick is inherently very powerful and can also be used to attack the hip joint.

*Inside Crescent Kick to the outside of a free elbow*

*Inside Crescent Kick to the inside of a free elbow*

*Crescent Kick to the hip of a developing Roundhouse Kick*

*A full-powered Crescent Stop Kick to the elbow of a developing punch will certainly do joint damage*

## Description

The Photos try to illustrate the little difference of execution when you attempt to crescent-kick a free elbow: at contact **you push the hips slightly forward**.

*Inside Crescent Kick to free elbow: push the hips for more joint damage*

## Typical Applications

The Figures below show an outside elbow attack, *without holding the arm in place*. You kick powerfully your opponent's guard at the elbow, and then you use a thrust of the hips to heel-kick his upper chest. It has the side effect of crushing his upper arm into his own body.

*Inside Crescent kick turns into Penetrating Heel Front Kick*

The next sets of Photos, below and at the top of next page, illustrate the most natural **follow-up to the Crescent Kick to a free elbow**: the Side Kick or the Back Kick. The compatibility comes from the fact that the Crescent Kick, after impact, turns into a natural Side or Side-back *Chamber*. The opponent's floating ribs have been uncovered by the arm strike and are open to a strong penetrating kick.

*Crescent-kick the elbow and side-kick the uncovered ribs*

*Same technique against a stick-wielding opponent, and with more of a Back Kick*

## Specific Training

Please refer to training tips for the classic (Inside) Crescent Kick, as presented in previous work. Mostly work on your flexibility and drill the *kick-through* and the *precision* on focus pads held by a partner.

## Self defense

The first set of Drawings illustrates how to deal with an assailant threatening you with a knife, poking and pulling back his knife just to intimidate. Wait for the next poke and **Crescent-kick the extending elbow**. Turn naturally into a Penetrating Side kick towards his lower ribs, as his armed arm has been thrown away. Bend away for safety, while side-kicking his front knee. Keep kicking him and do not let him take back the initiative. This is a Martial art drill but not a recommended technique in a real confrontation (*See our books about Krav Maga*).

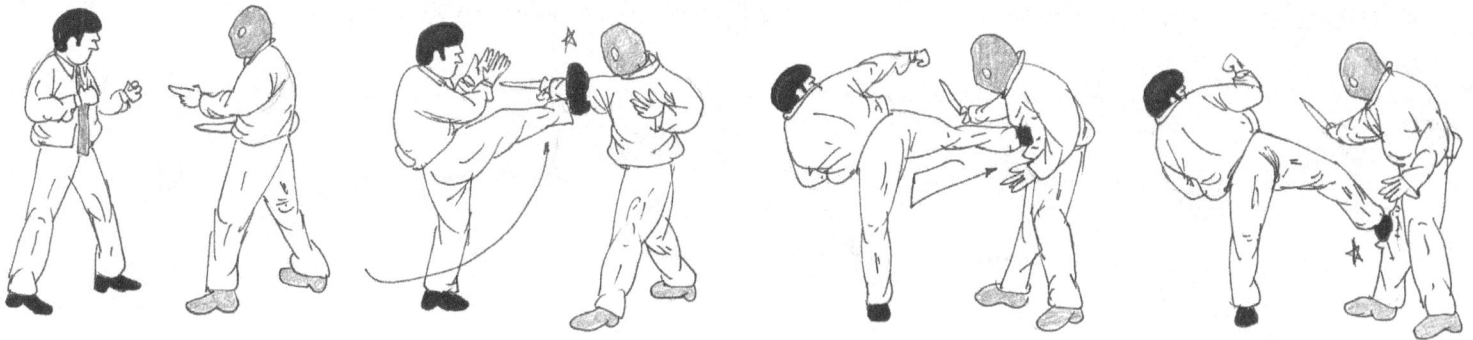

*Crescent Kick to an extending knife-arm and Side Kick follow-ups*

In the next example, you deal with an assailant holding a knife in front of him as a threat to you. Instead of cowering away, you surprise him by lunging at him to catch his armed wrist. Immediately launch a rear-leg Crescent Kick to the inside elbow of the caught (armed) arm. You could follow up with a Neck Hip Throw (*Koshi Guruma – Judo*) and finish him up on the ground (Keep hold of the armed wrist!).

*Crescent Kick to caught elbow, and follow-up*

The coming Drawing shows an interesting **variation on the ground**. As you lie down and your assailant tries to punch you from above, you crescent-kick his elbow from the outside *while crescent-kicking his wrist from the outside*. You could hold his wrist with your hands as well, but this makes for a fast and more protected way to hurt his joint. It is a sophisticated technique, but quite easy and very effective.

*An applied Double Crescent Joint Kick, surprising and very effective*

Another example will illustrate, again, that the **hip** can also be a valuable target, and that *front-leg Crescents* are possible. Against a classic stepping Punch attack, you retreat and block. Your Block becomes a grab as your rear leg comes back forward. Without interruption, you execute a **front-leg Crescent Kick to the hip joint** of the attacker.

*Applied front-leg Inside Crescent kick to the hip*

The coming combative is an extraordinary *variation on the Inside Crescent Joint Kick theme*. The Kick **to the knee of a caught kicking leg** is delivered with the inside knee or inside shin instead of the foot. It is easy to execute and the impact is as damaging to the joint as a regular Crescent Kick. And look at the follow-up! A joint-damaging throw of epic proportions that may look complicated but is in fact as easy to do as it is effective.

*Crescent Knee Strike to knee joint of scooped kicking leg and fantastic joint-damaging follow-up*

But another way to follow up on the previous Crescent Knee Strike is presented below. It is simpler and very effective as it becomes a Groin Kick. As soon as you have struck the immobilized knee with your own, you simply extend the leg to strike the exposed testicles from below.

*Crescent Knee Strike becomes Upward front kick to the groin*

With a little bit of imagination, the Crescent Joint Kick can be used *on the ground in joint locking maneuvers*. The whole point is to turn the switch in your mind, and setting an armlock can then become **a violent kicking maneuver**. In that way, the joint is already hurt while you set up a classic lock. This is more an attitude than a technical kick. The example *detailed at the top of next page* will make everything clear.

➡️

... With your opponent between your legs in ground grappling guard, you pivot to catch his rear shoulder and outer upper arm. Pull on his arm and pivot back while 'crescent-kicking' over it, therefore hurting the elbow. You can then catch your own foot to help pulling it over his elbow. Keep tight control of the locked arm and then kick forcefully straight over it for shoulder damage. Keep him locked if necessary.

3

★ KICK OUT ! 4

5 Ground grappling Applications of the Inside Crescent Join Kick and of the simple Front Joint Kick

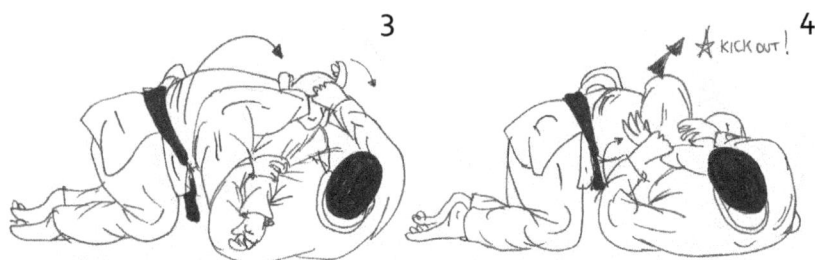

Another example of the **Grappling Ground use of the Inside Crescent Joint Kick** is presented in the Figures below. The principle stays the same, but, this time, the leg-extension follow-up is more of a *Side Kick*. The opponent is between your legs in Grappling Ground Guard, and he catches your lapel in order to better punch you with the other hand. You deflect the punch out while grabbing the wrist of his grabbing hand. Catch his punching arm and pivot while pulling it forward; this move also allows you to simultaneously elbow his head on the way. Keep pivoting with your whole body while keeping control of his extended punching arm and 'crescent-kick his elbow. The **Crescent Joint Kick** becomes a Side Kick that will further damage his elbow and shoulder. Keep him in armlock if necessary.

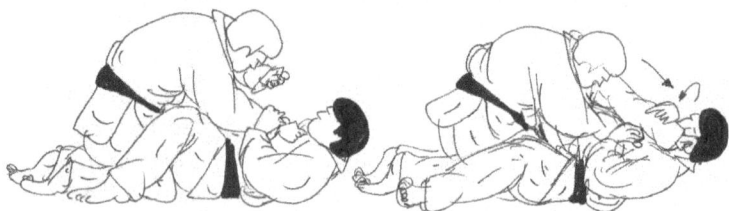

3

4

KICK OUT 5

*Ground Grappling version of a Crescent Joint Kick in armlock-mode, followed by a Side Kick extension for further damage*

As mentioned, Armlocks with the legs should be set up with 'kicking the joint' in mind for more damage and an easier set-up. The most common of Kicks in these instances is a variation of the Inside Crescent. Caution is warranted in training, though.

In our example below, you find yourself in Grappling Ground Guard with the opponent between your legs. Immediately envelop his arms from the outside, striking the elbows first if necessary. From this position of control, roll on your (right) side by pulling and pushing the arms. Use your left leg to kick his elbow that you maintain straight by pulling, then extend the leg violently for even more damage. You'll find yourself in *Juji Gatame* armlock position. Lift his wrist and push down with your leg on his elbow. Classic and simple, but requires training.

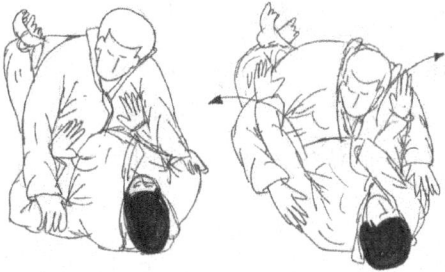

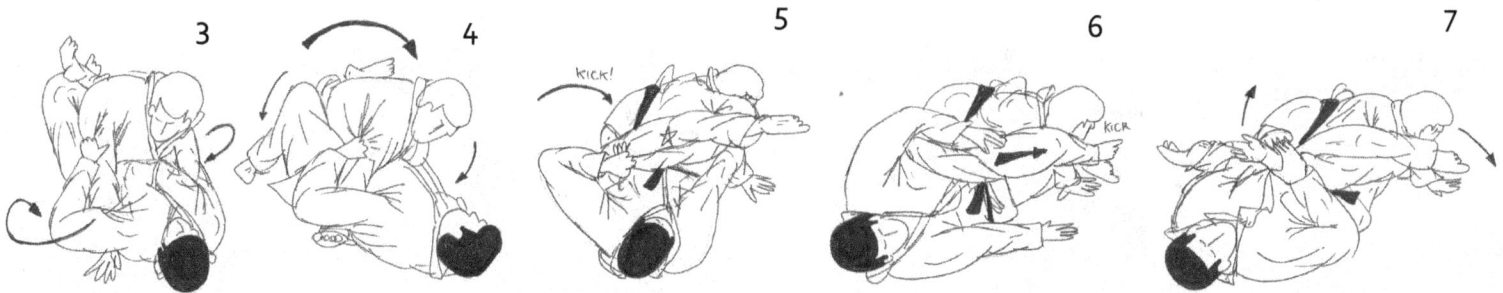

*Kick the elbow during the classic set-up of a ground arm-lock*

The following example shows in turn the set-up of an **armlock from a standing position over an opponent that has been just taken down.** Usually when you have thrown your opponent to the ground with a Judo-like Takedown, you still have control of one of his arms; sometimes the opponent has even still a grip on your lapel. Get close, pull his arm straight *and kick his elbow with your thigh* as you go over his head. The joint pain will help you set up the Scissor Armlock in which you block his elbow with the other thigh, either violently for damage or gradually for control.

*Thigh Kick to the elbow of a downed opponent to set up a standing Armlock*

**THE INSIDE CRESCENT KICK TO THE ELBOW** 109

And now comes an example of **the Elbow Kick to facilitate an Armlock from a standing position,** in Judo holding guard (*Kumi Kata*). Strike just above the knee of the opponent in order to hurt the join and push his leg back. Simultaneously, pull his arm down on the side of the attacked knee, and lift his other arm up. Keeping your foot on his knee you jump up and execute an **Assisted Flying Inside Crescent Kick against his lifted elbow.** Pull his arm and let yourself fall on the floor with the full weight of your leg on his elbow joint. Bend his arm and sit up in a painful Bent-arm Armlock that *BBJ* Artists call *Omoplata.*

*Assisted Flying Inside Crescent to elbow turns into Omoplata Armlock*

3    4    5

Another example of an 'Omoplata' set-up is described below, **for a ground-grappling situation.** You are in classic ground grappling guard and the opponent is between your legs. You catch his wrist at once and pull them out. Release your leg scissors and squeeze sideways for an **Inside Crescent to Downward Kick on his elbow** that you maintain extended. Sit up while encircling his elbow with your kicking leg. You have him in the classic (and painfully dangerous) Bent-arm Armlock; just remember to keep control of his body.

*Another Kick to Omoplata set-up in ground-fighting*

# 17. THE ROUNDHOUSE TO NECK CRANK KICK AND SIMILAR TECHNIQUES

## General

This is a very special technique coming from the South East Asian Arts. We present it as a Kick, because the way the Roundhouse Kick is delivered takes into account the following neck ensnaring. This is an interesting but difficult move, and very dangerous to boot. Practice slowly and with extreme caution.

## Description

The Figures shows how you kick *through* your opponent's head with a high Roundhouse or a high Straight-leg Roundhouse, causing him to bend back. You smoothly pivot with the hips while bending the leg, in order to catch his neck in the bend of your kicking knee. Ensnare his head as you pull him down and lower the foot into a tight neck-lock position. The opponent is now at your mercy, as you can hold his head while punching him or even attacking his eyes.

*The High Roundhouse kick to Neck Crank – a very dangerous technique*

## Typical Applications

As shown in the next set of Illustrations, *at the top of next page*, the best way to execute the technique is *after you have lowered his head height,* so that you can easily use the Straight-leg version of the Roundhouse Kick to make him bend backwards.

➤

... In this example, you evade your opponent's Roundhouse Kick by going rearwards and 'helping' his leg to keep going further. Control his lead hand for safety while low-kicking his landing leg at the knee, in order to cause him to buckle down. *That will lower the height of his head*. Immediately launch **a Straight-leg Roundhouse through his head,** with the other foot. Kick violently through and bend the leg to encircle his neck while pulling him down. Control the head with one hand (eventually with your fingers on his eyes), twist the thighs to squeeze the locked neck and eventually punch with the other hand.

*Low-kick the opponent's knee to lower the height of his head before 'low-kicking' it and ensnaring the neck in a crank*

There are several kicking techniques that lead to the **Neck Crank**. The following Illustrations show another way to get there after a Low Kick to buckle the opponent's knee. The beginning of the example could be identical to the previous one, with a rear evasion from a kick, but the way to get the Neck Crank is different. Instead of launching a Roundhouse kick with your other leg, you use the same leg to pass in front of the bucking opponent and then **hook-kick** his face. At contact you bend the leg around his neck for the crank. Your front hand catches his head from behind (hair grab if possible), as early as possible, to pull back and expose the throat.

*Hook Kick to Neck Crank*

But in fact, this is a *Neck Joint Attack* that you can launch **directly** if you can get your opponent down on his knees in front of you. This could be achieved for example with a simple Jab/Cross to Hooking Roundhouse to the back of the knee. Let your kicking leg pass in front of the opponent on his knees and violently ensnare his neck. Be careful not to 'shake' the hold in training!

*After any combo getting the opponent on his knees, hook-kick and bend-kick around his neck*

If you cannot get him down to execute the Kick, there is another option very typical of East-Asian Arts in general and of *Muay Thai Boran* in particular. Thai Artists are fond of 'monkey-like' **climbing techniques**; these are very spectacular but also very efficient. One must have been on the other end of it at least once to understand how surprisingly difficult to deal with these traditional techniques are. In the Illustrations below, you see how to evade a punching attack forward and out. You grab the punching arm and pull it forward, while placing your rear foot onto the opponent's hip (*A skilled practitioner will not simply lay his foot there but in fact stomp-kick the hip*). You will use your foot on his hip to climb over him and directly strike the side of his neck with your other thigh. Bend the leg on impact to ensnare the neck violently. As you have not let go of his grabbed punching arm, you can now also lock his elbow on your (climbing) leg gradually as a lock, or brusquely as a joint break. And you can compound all this with Downward Elbow Strikes on the top of his head. Keep your weight forward when you are sitting on him: this will make sure he crumbles forward and not backward, so that you can easily land on your feet.

*Execute the Neck Crank Kick when climbing on the opponent's shoulders: typical Thai style*

Another example of these East-Asian **Climbing techniques** is presented below, and it happens to be also damaging to the neck joints. The Illustrations below show how to close the gap to the opponent with a simple high Jab/Cross, in order to be able to place the rear foot violently on to the hip joint of the retreating opponent. This start of the 'climb' is somewhat of a Stomping Front Kick that also hurts the hip joint. At the same time, you grab the back of the adversary's neck (with the 'Cross' hand) and pull it violently towards you. That both hurts and helps you to climb. Jump up with a 'flying' Knee Strike to his chin while keeping the pull on his neck. This is very bad for the vertebrae and will be compounded by an additional and nearly-simultaneous Downward Elbow Strike to the top of his head. Let go and land, ready to follow up on your shaken opponent.

*Another neck-damaging Climbing Technique: Flying Knee and Vertical Elbow*

We shall now present another acrobatic attack of the neck joint, derived from the *Sacrifice Twin Inside Crescent Flying Kick* already encountered in previous books. The technique is spectacular and much easier to succeed with than it may seem. From a classic *Judo* holding guard (*Kumi Kata*), you jump with a Twin Inside Crescent Kick while pulling yourself on your holds of him. Try to hit the side of his neck (on the side you hold his lapel) and his elbow (on the side he holds your lapel). Keep your holds tight *and twist when falling down in order to keep a 'kicking' pressure on the side of his neck*. Bend the leg behind his neck and hook over the foot with your other leg to place him in a powerful Neck Lock. *Remember that his extended arm pressing on his carotids is key to the lock success.* Use both hands to pull his head down and make the Choke/Neck lock more effective.

*Twin Inside Crescent Assisted Flying Kick to elbow and neck, followed by mean Leg Choke*

*A variation of this important technique* is presented below. In that case, you will kick over his head with one leg, the other hitting his elbow or his ribs. The idea is to come back once the head overtaken, in order to strike the neck from the other side! As you have kept your holds, the arm that was holding your lapel is extended in Armlock position as you land. Simple, efficient and surprising.

*A variation of the Twin Flying Kick leading to a Neck Strike and a classic Armlock*

*An equivalent of this technique in ground-fighting* is presented below. It is simple and fiendishly effective. You have thrown your opponent to the ground with some Judo-like Takedown and he still holds your lapel while you hold his sleeve. Classic end-position. **Immediately strike the side of his neck,** on his unprotected side, with something akin to a *Hooking Inside Crescent.* Strike hard and *through.* Simultaneously pull his arm straight up. Hook the leg behind his neck and fall on him with all your weight, pushing his extended arm over his neck and face. Strangle and lock him by using your body weight to push his arm down and your leg squeezing his neck. You can compound the lock by pulling his head up with your hands. Extreme caution is required in training!!

*Hook the neck of an opponent thrown to the ground and set up Neck Lock*

***Another way to attack the neck on the way to an armlock*** is presented in the Figures below. The attacker grabs your lapel aggressively. You immediately strike his elbow into hyperextension: the angle of the strike depends on the grab itself but is easy to figure intuitively. Anyway, strike violently and then grab the weakened arm. Simultaneously you yourself will grab his lapel. Pull him towards you while striking his hip joint with a Kick that is in fact a *Reverse Shin Kick*. Kick hard and jump up, crossing in front of his head with your foot. Come back *to strike his neck in something akin to a Downward Hook Kick*. Kick *through* while twisting in the air and keeping full control of his extended grabbing arm. He will fall to the floor in classic *Juji Gatame* Armlock. Lift your hips and pull his wrist down.

*Hooking Downward Neck Assisted Jumping Kick for the set-up of a classic ground Armlock*

And we'll conclude with another spectacular climbing technique, ***resulting in two Inside Crescent Strikes to both sides of the neck***. From a classic *Judo* standing holding guard (*Kumi Kata*), you strike the opponent's hip with a Stomping Front Kick that becomes an Assist for your climb. Jump up by using his hip or upper thigh as a step and *strike the side of his neck* with your thigh or knee in an Inside Crescent move. Leave your leg on his neck and *repeat the kicking move on the other side* while keeping your strong holds of his sleeve and lapel. Let you fall on the ground while extending his (lapel-grabbing) hand. Your hips and body weight will push his elbow down while your hands will pull his wrist up. You both will end on the floor, with your holding him in a powerful Armlock position, and with his neck bruised. See Illustrations at the top of next page. ➡️

**THE ROUNDHOUSE TO NECK CRANK KICK**

*Climbing Neck Kicks and Armlock finish, from Judo stance*

# If your opponent is of choleric temper, irritate him.
## ~Sun Tzu

# 18. THE DOWNWARD HEEL KICK TO THE NECK

## General

As we have just seen, the neck is a joint, therefore a target, and a very dangerous one at that. It is one of the natural targets of the basic **Downward Heel Kick** (or *Axe Kick*), as already presented in our work about *Essential Kicks*. This is a potentially lethal technique to be practiced with extreme caution. In any situation in which the opponent presents the back of his neck as a target, this hard-to-block Kick becomes highly relevant.

*Downward Heel Kick the neck of a bent-over opponent whenever possible*

## Description

The Photos below show a classic combination illustrating the rationale behind the Kick: A Roundhouse Kick to the solar plexus will cause your opponent to bend over, opening the back of his neck to a **Downward Heel strike**. Be extremely careful in practice.

*Kick to cause the opponent to bend over and Axe-kick his offered neck*

## Typical Applications

The principle stays the same in the special application presented in the Drawings *at the top of next page*: Evade (down, forward and out) a full-step lunge punch, while simultaneously roundhouse-elbowing your opponent's exposed ribs. This may seem a convoluted technique but it is surprisingly easy and efficient if you have honed your preemptive striking instincts. After the naturally-following Knee Strike, *your bent-over opponent's back neck can easily be downward-heel-kicked.*

➡️

*A special Stop Strike that will bend the opponent over for the Downward Kick*

*Another way* to follow up with the **Downward Kick** after the same Elbow Stop Strike is presented in the Figures below. After the low Elbow Strike, you stand up and attack his head with a Hook Punch. Strike through with all you have and keep the momentum for an Outside Crescent Spin-back Kick that will become a **diagonal Downward Heel** to the neck of the crouching opponent.

*Another sequence based on the previous surprise Stop Strike*

## Specific Training

The reader is invited to consult 'The Essential Book of Martial Arts Kicks' for training drills for the classic Downward Heel Kick. This one is the same, but simply targeting the neck.

## Self defense

The last Figures shows the use of the technique if you have used **an Arm-lock to cause him to bend down**. In the example, your assailant grabs your collar from behind, and you Rear-low-kick his shin to soften him up before you twist under his grab. Get hold of his grabbing hand and develop the classical Tai-jitsu Arm-lock illustrated. Kick down on his neck as soon as he bends down.

*A great Kick if you can use an Arm-lock to make the opponent bend down and present his neck*

# 19. THE DOWNWARD HEEL KICK TO ARM-LOCKED ELBOW AND SCISSOR LOCK

## General

This is a classic Arm-lock set-up found in *Ju-jitsu* and in many Korean Arts. The entry can be mild or it can be a full devastating Joint Kick, as deemed by the circumstances. The Kick, in itself, is a simple **Downward Heel Kick** directed at a controlled elbow. This is a very effective and complete technique, much loved by the author. It can be capped by simply sitting on the opponent stretched elbow, or in a more sophisticated **Scissor Arm-lock**.

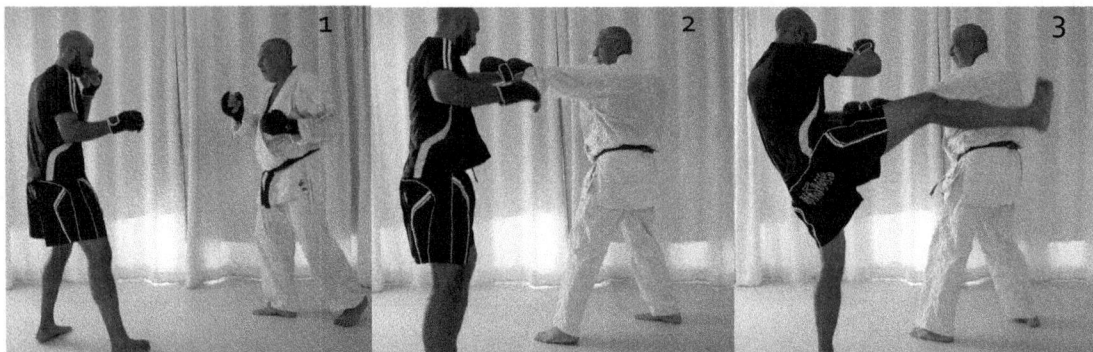

The Downward Heel Kick to Elbow, followed by 'sitting-on-the-elbow' Lock

## Description

The Drawings *at the top of next page* illustrate the applied technique **capped with the Scissor Lock**. The example shows how to block a Reverse Punch and get hold of the opponent's wrist. You then twist the wrist while pulling the arm straight, and you lift the front leg high for a *Downward 'Axe' Heel Kick to the exposed elbow*. You do not connect with the heel of course, but with the back of the thigh or of the calf. Keep hold of the wrist for the naturally following and well-illustrated *Scissor Arm-lock*. ➡

*Block and grab the opponent's wrist and kick; finish by squeezing the elbow in an Armlock between your thighs*

## Key Points

- Kick *through*, just thinking of lowering the foot to the floor.
- *Twist the wrist* in order to present the opponent's elbow upwards.
- *Pull the arm while kicking*. For maximum damage, you can pull the wrist up at impact.
- The Scissor Lock will be more effective if *compounded with a Wrist Lock* (See following section).

## Typical Applications

The next Drawings show that this is the maneuver of choice *after you have placed your opponent in a Wrist Lock*. In this example, you turn a straight wrist grab into a classic *Aiki-jitsu* Wrist-lock. After a fast Upward Front Kick to his bending-down face, you deliver the **Downward Heel Kick through his elbow**. You will then compound the 2 possible endings: you first execute a brusque and violent Scissor Lock to damage the joint, and then only you conclude by sitting (with all your weight) on his upper arm for Lock control.

*Same technique from a wrist grab, but preceded by a 'mollifying' Front Kick and followed by both locking follow-ups*

The last Drawings of the section will show *a different finish* to the technique. As your opponent grabs your lapels, you soccer-front-kick his shin while pinning his wrists. Make use of the effect of the kick for one hand to grab the wrist holding the opposite lapel, in a classic wrist-lock release. *You use your whole body* to bring him into Arm-lock position. Strike the extended elbow with your palm to further mollify him. You can then easily execute the Joint Kick and 'sit' on his upper arm (Make sure his elbow joint points upwards). After a very natural Small Back Hook Kick to the face, you can sit on your knee while twisting his wrist and therefore arm-locking his elbow on the back of your thigh. Twist your body to strain his shoulder as well, get hold of his chin and add a neck crank to all his troubles.

1    2    3

*Lapel Grab Release capped with Downward Heel Joint Kick and painful Submission*

4    5    6    7

8    9    10    11

## Self defense

We shall start the Self Defense Applications with a **Wrist Grab Release**. Pull the grabbed wrist and use his counter-pulling reaction to envelop and counter-grab his own wrist. All the while, you are already executing an *Inside Crescent Kick* to his head. Pull on his arm as the leg comes down, so that contact will be with the extended elbow. Just like for the previous application, you can sit brusquely on his arm and strike his head with a Small Back Hook Kick while keeping control. See Figures.

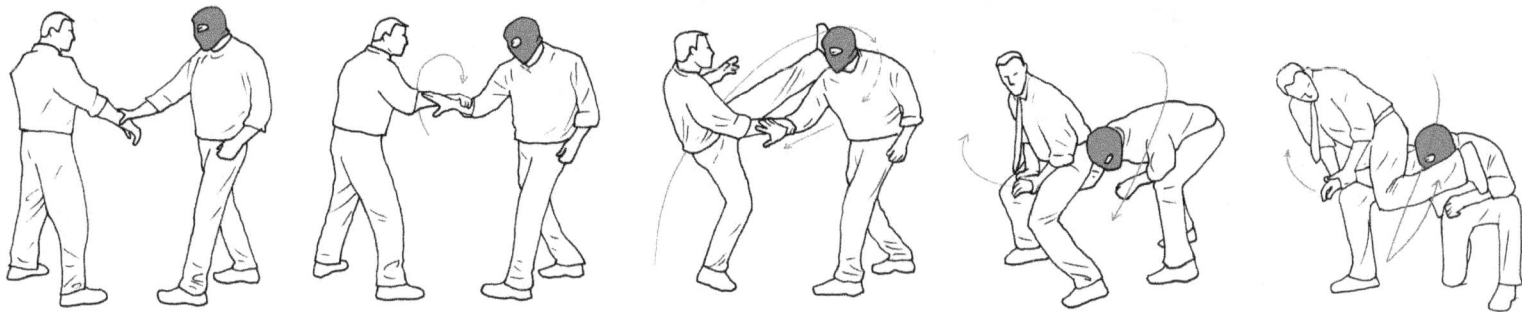

*Wrist Grab release and Crescent to Downward Joint kick*

The coming Drawings illustrate a **variation of the Kick executed more to your opponent's front side** and particularly suitable to follow a "*Hakkoryu*- type of Wrist-lock. Against a lapel grab, execute the classic escape into this "side-down" Wrist-lock which causes the opponent to kneel in pain in front of you. You will then *Upward-front-kick* his chin to lift the leg, and then strike down onto his elbow as you pull the arm. The opponent will be seriously hurt and lying down on his belly in front of you. Following up should be pretty easy.

*Variation of the Kick with an Upward Front Kick on the way up and the Downward Kick frontally on the elbow of an arm maintained by a 'side' Wrist lock*

We shall now present Figures that show an *interesting finish to the technique*, ending in a classical *Judo Ne-waza* Arm-lock. Against a knife stab to the belly (that you can cause with a head feint), you evade and get hold of the armed wrist from above. Turn it into a classical Wrist Lock (both thumbs on the back of his hand) *by using your whole body* for the twist. The body twist will help the start of the powerful Kick. Smash down his elbow joint and then drop immediately on your knees, *with your whole body weight on his arm*. Keep hold of his wrist and extend your leg in front of his, as you roll on your side to throw him forward. He'll be falling on his back, caught in classical Arm-lock position (*Juji Gatame - Judo*), under your full control.

**1    2    3    4**

*Wrist Lock against Knife Stab is compounded by a Downward Kick to the elbow and finished with the set-up of a Judo Ground Armlock*

**5    6    7    8    9**

And now a traditional *Tai-Jitsu* exercise ending with our Kick. The Drawings show a classical Inside block of a traditional Stepping Punch. The elbow of the Blocking arm will go up fast to hit the opponent's head and mollify him for a Wrist-lock grab. As soon as the opponent bends to alleviate or prevent the pain, you *Crescent-kick his elbow* going up, and *Downward-kick it* on the way down. Of course, you pivot when lowering the leg to be in position for either sitting on his elbow or scissor-locking it.

*The Downward Kick to elbow extended by a lock, in a traditional training set*

The next example underlines that **both legs can be used to kick down onto the extended elbow**: the Kick needs not necessarily be Inside-Crescent-like. The Drawings show how to fake a jabbing punch in order to get control of the opponent's front hand. Do not let go of the hand while front-kicking his lower abdomen and landing with a punch to the face. Grab the back of his neck to pull his face into a Knee Strike, while lifting his grabbed hand up. You will then lift you kneeing leg as high as possible, straight, and lower it as an axe on to the opponent's extended upper arm. Pull on the wrist to cause maximum elbow joint damage, and strive to land the foot of the kicking leg onto the opponent's hands (*that go naturally to the floor to slow his going to the floor*).

*Axe Kick to the extended elbow* **with the front leg**

The coming variation is extremely effective and, in fact, **gets rid of the need for a full and orthodox 'Axe Kick'**: you just lift the leg just *enough to go over the caught kicking leg*, and you use your bottom and whole-body weight to sit violently on his extended knee. Simple and viciously efficient!

*Forget the Downward Kick and simply sit on the extended knee*

**THE DOWNWARD HEEL KICK TO ARM-LOCKED ELBOW**

The last Drawings illustrate *a different execution of the Downward Kick,* followed by a great **Armlock Takedown** that is much easier to execute than it may look. In our example, your assailant grabs your lapel. Catch his grabbing sleeve and go over his arm with your other hand in order to grab his rear shoulder. You should here mollify him with a groin kick or knee strike, but we have not illustrated it to keep the sequence flowing. Pull on his arm with both hands in order to make the opponent bend forward, and immediately place your knee over his shoulder (*Roundhouse Chamber-style*). This is a more economical way to get over his shoulder, and you can still lower the leg forcefully after you have cleared the shoulder area. The result is similar to a Downward Heel to the elbow, though probably less powerful. The follow-up presented is interesting though: You place the leg that has just struck the extended elbow between the assailant's legs in order to hook his knee. Let yourself fall backwards in a Roll while lifting the hooking leg and while pulling on his arm. He should be thrown over you and land in perfect position for a mean classic *Juji Gatame* Armlock on his already hurting elbow.

*Downward Elbow Kick from Roundhouse Chamber, followed by a mean Armlock Takedown*

## 20. THE DOWNWARD HOOK KICK TO EXTENDED KICKING KNEE

### General

This is a very sophisticated Joint Kick, *totally dependent on perfect timing* for maximum joint damage effect. If timing is off, this is still a great Block Kick maneuver, but without joint-damage potential. The Kick in itself is a basic **Downward Hook Kick** (see 'Essential Kicks') delivered **on to an incoming knee**, in a "hooking" way. As the opponent's leg is not hold, speed and angle of attack are of the essence. The Kick can be executed with the front or the rear leg, but there will always be some evading footwork involved.

### Description

The most common example of the technique is presented in the coming Figures: a rear-leg Kick against a Side Kick. As your opponent launches a Hopping front-leg Side Kick from an opposite stance, you step _forward and outside_ the centerline. The rear leg develops a high Hook Kick *over* the opponent's leg, and then **hooks down onto the extending/extended knee, while bending on contact** ("*hooking*"). You have to kick _through_ to maximize joint damage and then you should follow up. A natural way to do so would be to relaunch the kicking leg in a high Roundhouse, as the ending position of the Downward Hook Kick is very close to a classic Roundhouse Chamber.

*The Downward Hook Kick to the knee of a developing Side Kick*

### Key Points

- The *Downward Hook Kick should ideally connect as the opponent's leg reaches full extension.*
- Kick *through* and start *hooking* ,-bending the leg-, at contact.
- Use full *body weight* to lower the leg through the knee.
- *Always follow up.*

## Typical Application

The next Drawings show a **front-leg version**, against a Front Kick attack. Your opponent, in opposite stance, launches a powerful rear-leg Penetrating Front Kick. You hop directly sideways and forward into an *Evading High Hook Kick* chamber, and you will lower the leg forcefully *through* his incoming knee. Follow up, for example by letting your kicking foot rebound on the floor for a high Roundhouse.

*Front-leg Evading Downward Hook Kick through the knee of a developing Front Kick*

## Specific Training

- Drill the applications presented for *timing*; start slowly. *Timing* is the key of this technique.
- Refer to '*The Essential Book of Martial arts Kicks*' for drills of the basic Downward Hook Kick.

## Self defense

The last set of Illustrations shows another example of t*he front-leg version of the Kick*, this time against a rear-leg Roundhouse from identical stances. After kicking through his knee, you can follow up with a Jab that precedes a rebounding high Roundhouse.

1       2

*Same stances, front-leg version,*
*against rear-leg Roundhouse*

3       4       5

## Success at anything will always come down to this: Focus & Effort, and we control both.
### ~Dwayne Johnson

## 21.  THE BACK HOOK KICK TO STANDING KNEE

### General

This is again a "sweep-looking" Kick. The technique presented will be identical to well-known Reaping Takedowns. But the difference is **in the emphasis, in the mindset and in the point of impact**. You should kick the knee cap *straight and hard*, with the purpose of hurting the joint. And only in a second stage should you eventually worry about lifting the leg to take him down. This is a very specific Kick against kicking attacks, but if relevant to the situation, it is a devastating maneuver: Not only do you hurt the knee joint, but you also cause the opponent to fall hard on his face.

### Description

The coming Figures show the *classic* execution of the Kick against a Spin-back Hook Kick. As your opponent spins back, you lunge diagonally forward close to him and his axis of pivot. You can then catch his leg and reap his standing leg with 'joint attack' in mind. Once you have kicked brusquely *through* his knee joint, you can concentrate on maximizing the impact of his fall. Lift him high and push him down head first.

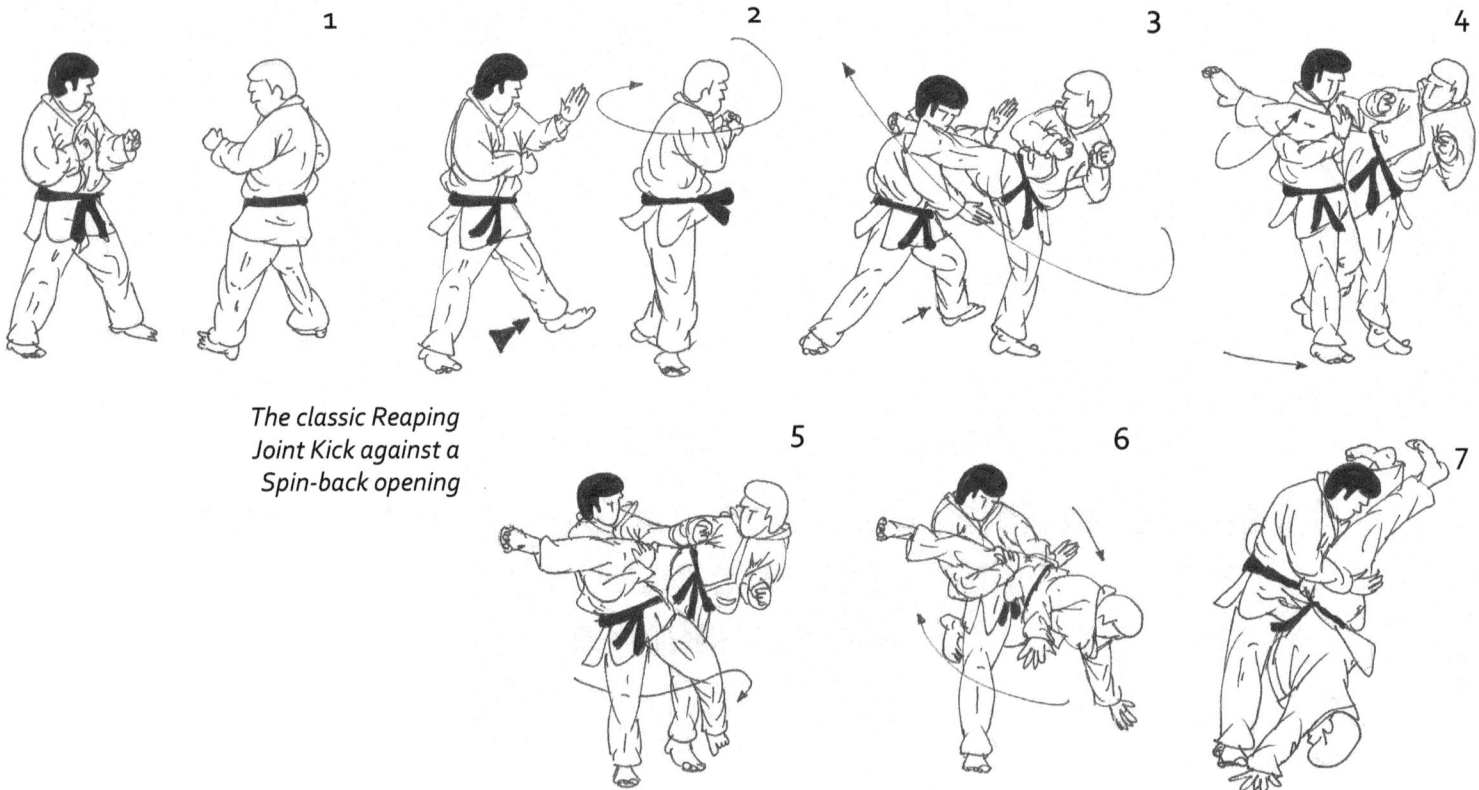

1  2  3  4

*The classic Reaping Joint Kick against a Spin-back opening*

5  6  7

## Key Points

- Kick *through*, do not sweep.
- Hit the kneecap *from the front, straight, not up*. Use the calf.
- *Do not lift the opponent* during the Kick, as you would do for a sweep.

## Typical Application

The next Drawings show the entry *against a front-leg Side Kick* attack. Evade forward and out, and catch the leg by scooping with the rear hand. Cross-step to get close while pulling and lifting the leg. Hook-kick back *directly through to the knee* to damage it. Only at impact, start twisting the body to cause the subsequent Takedown.

*The Reaping Joint Kick against a front-leg Side Kick*

3   4   5   6

## Self defense

The first Illustrations, at the top of next page, will show the application *against a Penetrating Front Kick*. All principles are identical.

➤

*The Reaping Joint Kick against a Front Kick*

The last set of Drawings will show a **variation of the Kick that attacks the front leg of an opponent in front of you**. It is a Takedown that also attempts to hurt the joint by causing a hyperextension. It is an interesting little technique that works well as a Takedown, but does not cause extensive joint damage. You can set it up easily by lunging forward with a high Jab/Cross combo. The Cross turns into a lapel or shoulder grab that pushes him back while your rear leg comes to hook into his lower leg from behind. Kick through and                use your body to push.

1                    2

*A nice and surprising Takedown: Lunge and hook-kick the opponent's front lower leg from behind*

3                    4                    5

# 22. THE SHIN FRONT PUSH KICK AS A JOINT KICK

## General

This is a very special Kick, nearly anecdotal, but potentially useful in close quarters fighting. The basic version is presented in our book about *Stop Kicks* and is quite commonly used in *Muay Thai*. To become a successful Joint Kick, it requires technique, mindset and timing, as the attacked leg must be pinned down. But you can then connect at any point between the hip and the knee to cause overall joint damage.

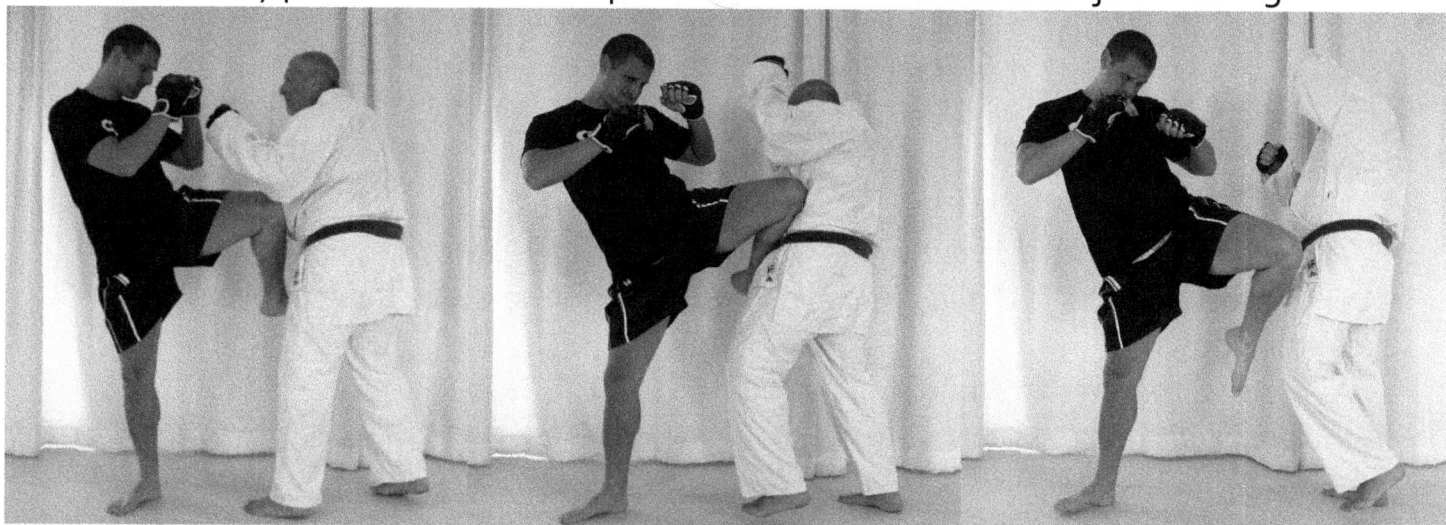

*The classic Shin Front Push Stop Kick targeting the lower ribs or hip*

*The front-leg Shin Front Push Stop Kick*

## Description

The coming Illustrations, at the top of next page, show the technical execution of the kick *as a Joint Kick*. In close combat, you lift the leg as if delivering a Roundhouse Knee Strike at belt level in front of the opponent. As soon as you are over his front thigh you thrust the hips forward and kick *down* with the shin just above the knee. You thus straighten his leg and nail his heel to the floor. Kick **through** with breaking his knee in mind. This as much a mindset than a technical difference.

➤

*The Joint Kick version of the Shin Front Pushing Stop Kick*

## Key Points

- Thrust the hips and use *your whole body weight* to kick down.
- The thrust must be *fast and explosive* to prevent him to move the front foot before it is stuck down.
- Aim *above the knee* to straighten his leg.
- Kick *through*.

## Typical Application

The coming Drawings illustrate the use of the Kick as a Joint-hurting Stop Kick **against a punching attack**. Your opponent launches a Cross that you block while hopping forward in Shin Pushing Kick mode. But you aim at the hip joint to both stop him and cause joint damage. You can follow up with a series of Elbow Strikes.

*Stop-kicking the hip joint will both stop an attack and cause joint damage*

## Self defense

The next Figures show how to use the Kick in a **double wrist grab defense**. As your assailant grabs both your wrists, you retreat back and lower your gravity center, all the while encircling his wrists. In typical *Tai Chi* fashion or as per basic *Judo* principles, you round up your retreat seamlessly *back into a forward movement,* just as he reacts instinctively to pull you back towards him. You open the arms as you explode forward into the Kick. You can then push down on his thigh as his heel is glued to the ground. Put your *whole body weight* into it until he is on the ground with your knee on his thigh, still controlling his wrists. Stand up fast and stomp his ankle.

*Use the Kick against a double wrist grab, and keep pushing down until he is on the ground with all your body weight on his joint*

And the last set of Photos will illustrate the simple straightforward technique against a Jab.

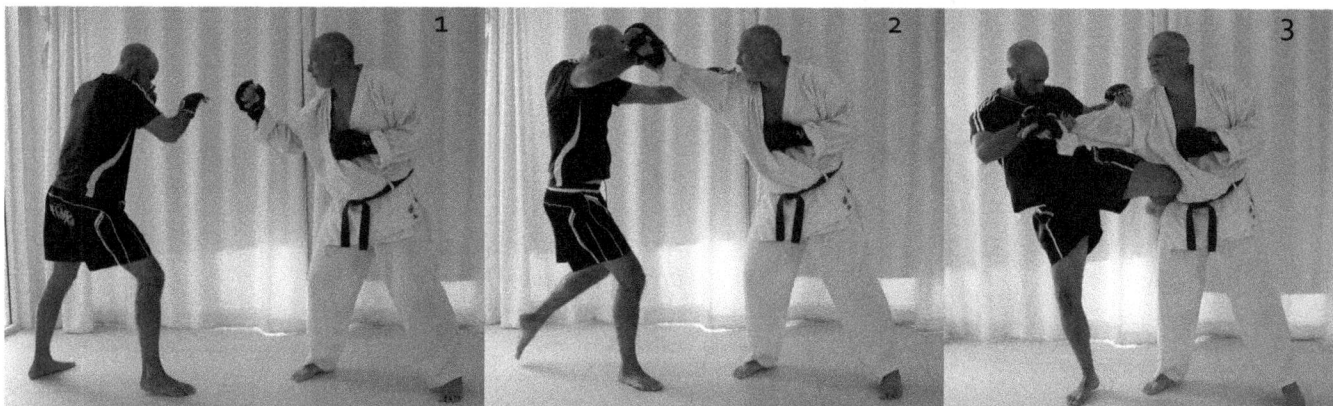

*Applied Shin Front Kick to the hip joint*

**THE SHIN FRONT PUSH KICK AS A JOINT KICK**   137

# 23. THE FACE STOMP WITH ARM BREAK

## General

This is not a pure Joint Kick, but still a very effective technique from old *Ju-Jitsu* that I love. It was a natural real-life follow-up to takedowns. After throwing your opponent to the ground while keeping control of one of his arms, you'd **simultaneously stomp his head and break the elbow** by pulling energetically the controlled arm against the stomping leg. Pretty gruesome. It is easier to try than to describe technically. Just try slowly and gradually faster with a partner, and you'll get the hang of it in no time.

## Description

The first set of Drawings illustrates the technique after a typical Shoulder Throw (*Ippon Soei Nage – Judo*). The Arm Break comes simultaneously with the Head Stomp. Stomp *through* the head and pull his elbow *through* your thigh.

Arm-breaking Head stomp after a Shoulder Throw; in dealing with an overhead stick attack

## Typical Application

As an application, we shall present in the next Drawings the execution of a Shoulder Wheel Takedown (*Kata Guruma- Judo*) against a stick attack. Our arm breaking techniques comes as the assailant lands hard on the floor.

**1**

**2**

**3**

*Arm-breaking Head Stomp after Kata Guruma*

**4**

**5**

# No battle plan survives contact with the enemy.
# ~Colin Powell

# 24. THE FLYING KNEE STOMP

## General

This is a **Flying Stomp Kick** (as described in 'Low Kicks') but one that specifically targets the thigh of the opponent, just above the knee. It is a very special technique, but that can be extremely surprising and damaging. Your knees protect your body while you jump high up and aggressively towards your opponent, and the last thing he will expect is an attack to his lower limbs. You will then use your whole body weight to crush his leg all the way into the floor. Of course, you should take into account that you could lose your balance after the stomp and would have to roll if necessary.

This is a nice technique to drill, even if you will never use it. The protected jump towards the opponent will teach you lots about going forward, and the balancing act after the stomp will teach you to react according to the circumstances.

## Description

The coming Figures show how you jump up and forward towards your opponent. Once

both knees are in the air you stomp down with one foot onto his front thigh, just above the knee. It works best if you can catch his knee slightly bent, as he instinctively retreats from your jump. You kick while landing with your whole body weight, and he should fall on the floor under you. Try to land with your non-kicking foot just after impact. Should you lose your balance upon landing, you should reception yourself with a 'Judo' Roll and stand back up immediately (unless you are good at 'Ground Kicks').

3    4    5    6

*The basic Flying Knee Stomp*

## Typical Application

The next set of Drawings illustrates **(1)** how to <u>"fix" him in place</u> before you jump, and **(2)** that you can also deliver <u>Two</u> Kicks while going down. In the example, you evade and catch your assailant's Jab attack. You will then pull his arm forward, as you rear-leg front-kick his open ribs. Lower the kicking leg and use his arm to help you jump up. Stomp with one kick, and then with the other as you go down. Follow up.

1        2        3

*Double Flying Stomp Kick Application*

4        5        6        7

## Illustrative Photos

*The regular basic Flying Stomp Kick*

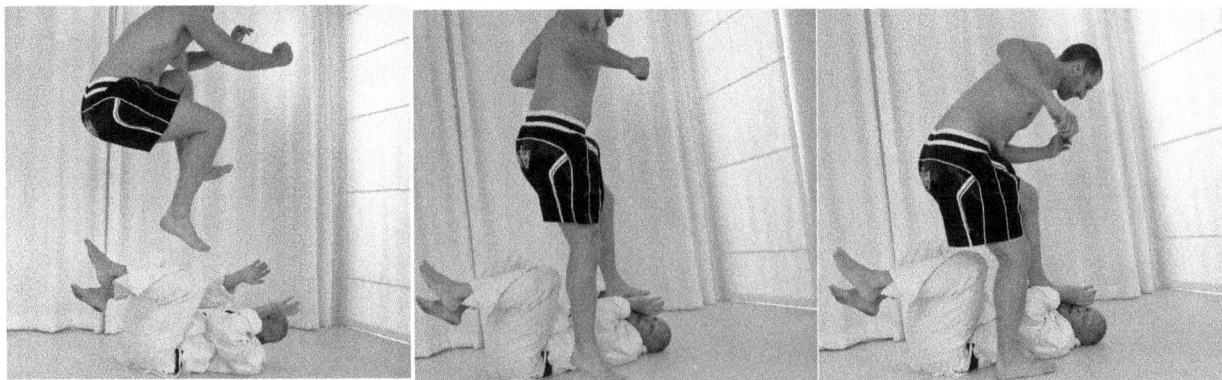

# 25. THE STRAIGHT LEG BACK SWEEPING KICK

*(Old Ju-Jitsu versions of: Uchi Mata, O Soto Gari, Harai Goshi)*

## General

This technique, again, is not truly a full Kick, but it is important to present the rationale behind it. We shall present the way classical *Judo* throws used today in training and in sport competition, were executed in the old realistic *Ju-Jitsu*. The beautiful leg sweeps of today's *Judo* were then vicious Kicks to the joint that were turning into finishing throws. The distinction is real, as we shall show, but it is also a lot in the mindset. Once you will start practicing the throws, you will be able to see and understand how a simple change of angle turns a sweep into a strike to the joint first. In fact, if you drill with that mindset, it will become much clearer than my poor text.

Here come, below and on next page, the classic *Judo* Takedowns, as practiced today: *Uchi Mata* (Inside Thigh Sweep), *O Soto Gari* (Outside Leg Reap) and *Harai Goshi* (Sweeping Hip Throw). Notice that they all require a powerful throwing of the straightened leg rearwards, *a straight-leg Back Kick of sorts.*

*Judo's Uchi Mata Takedown*

*Classic O Soto Gari Takedown*

*My favorite: Harai Goshi as executed in sport Judo*

## Description

And now, the nasty versions:

**The first set of Figures** shows how *Uchi Mata* does not sweep the inside thigh, **but kicks the knee**. Hit the front of the knee *straight on with the mindset of hurting the joint*. The reader is invited to note that the 'kick' could also aim for the groin (which is not a joint, obviously), or even better, it could do a double whammy: hit the knee, then gets in to go for the groin and the subsequent Takedown.

*The set-up for an 'Uchi Mata'-type Joint attack and Takedown*

**The second set of Drawings** shows how *O Soto Gari* was executed as a *Straight-leg Kick to the side of the knee*, later turning into a glide and then the full leg Reap. The principle is simple and practice will make it easily clear.

*O Soto Gari can hurt the knee joint if necessary*

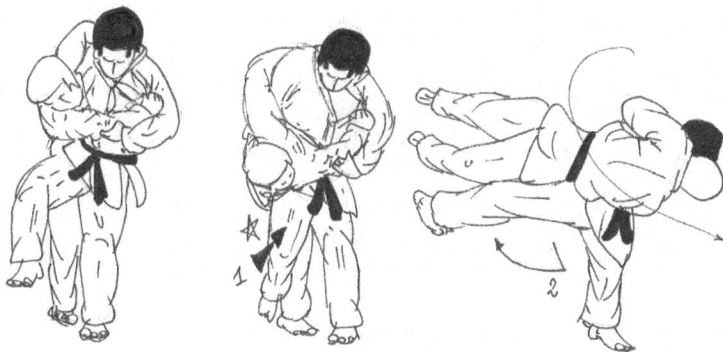

And the Illustrations beside show how *Harai Goshi* can be executed: you kind of *stomp rearwards to hit the opponent's knee straight on with your thigh* to hurt his knee. You can then flow into a higher sweeping 'kick' to complete the classic hip Takedown.

*Harai Goshi to the knee first, then higher*

## Typical Applications

There are of course, many applications of those hybrid techniques, and the reader will find his own adaptations of these principles. The coming Figures illustrate a defense against an **attempted Bear Hug from the front**. The example shows how to go from a groin knee strike/head butt combo, into a kick to the side of the knee, and then into classic *Harai Goshi*. Each one of the strikes allows you to get into position for the final throw. Of course, you may need to follow up.

*Knee-hurting Harai Goshi to conclude a Bear hug defense*

The coming Illustrations, at the top of next page, will show in turn how to use a knee-hurting Outer Reap Takedown *against a kicking attack*. The Drawings show how to evade diagonally forward a full-powered rear-leg Penetrating Front Kick and grab the opponent. From there you can easily keep him off-balance and kick *the side knee of his standing leg*. After the Joint Kick you can flow easily into the classic *O Soto Gari* Takedown.

*Evade kick, grab and execute the full knee-hurting Takedown*

## Self defense

The last set of Figures will show how to use the *Uchi Mata* variation in a **Clinch** situation. You have to make sure you achieve a clinching position in which you have an *over-hook*. As he clinches, push him away on your under-hook side and pivot to place your hip in between. Deliver immediately an *"Uchi Mata Kick"* to his knee, with the mindset of hurting the joint. Pivot back to punch him in the face as he is off-balance, and now repeat the Uchi Mata, this time kicking *up into his groin*.

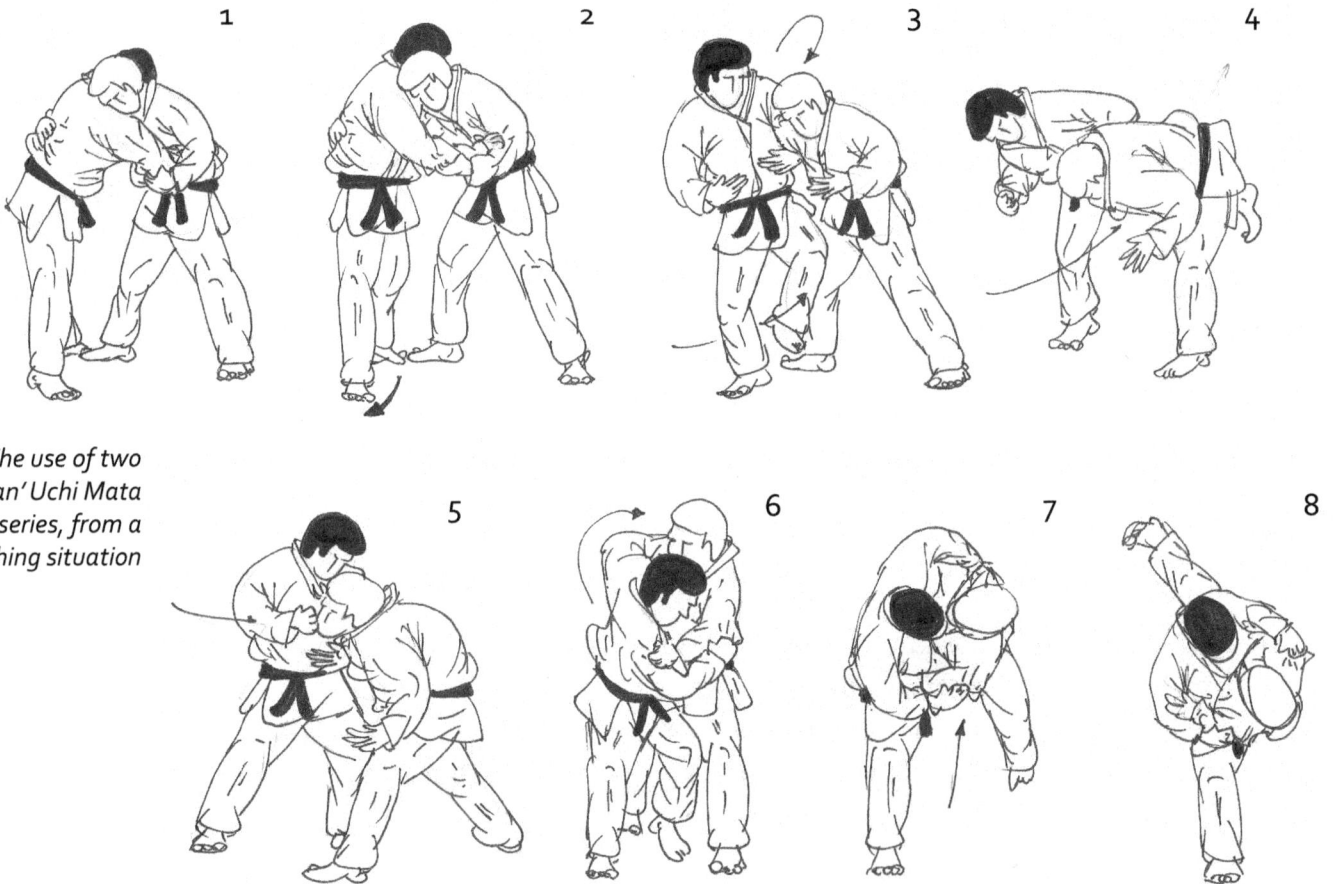

*The use of two 'mean' Uchi Mata in series, from a Clinching situation*

# 26.  THE HIP SWEEP KICK

## General

This move is, again, not a kick in the fullest sense: it is delivered as a Straight-leg Kick and does hurt the opponent's hip joint, but the primary purpose of the maneuver is to sweep the opponent off his feet. It is a great move though, very effective once mastered, causing both physical and mental damage to the opponent. This is a technique I used a lot as a young fighter against "fleeing" opponents, causing them a hard fall, hip pain, a follow-up punch to the ground and total mental domination. The maneuver requires perfect timing on a moving opponent, preferably fleeing rearwards.

## Description

The Kick is only relevant in a dynamic situation, and will be presented as such. The coming Drawings illustrate the classic "jab" entry.  Facing a "retreating" opponent, you hop forward with a deep Jab towards his eyes and follow him with a cross-step, keeping your hands up in his vision field. As he pulls back his front leg, you "go" together with his leg and *kick through his hip with your upper thigh*. The Kick is akin to a straight-leg Front Kick. You push your hips forward to put your whole body into the Kick and stick as much as possible to your opponent's body. This causes your opponent's leg to lift up, and he will fall from pretty high. As he falls, control his legs as you punch him down.

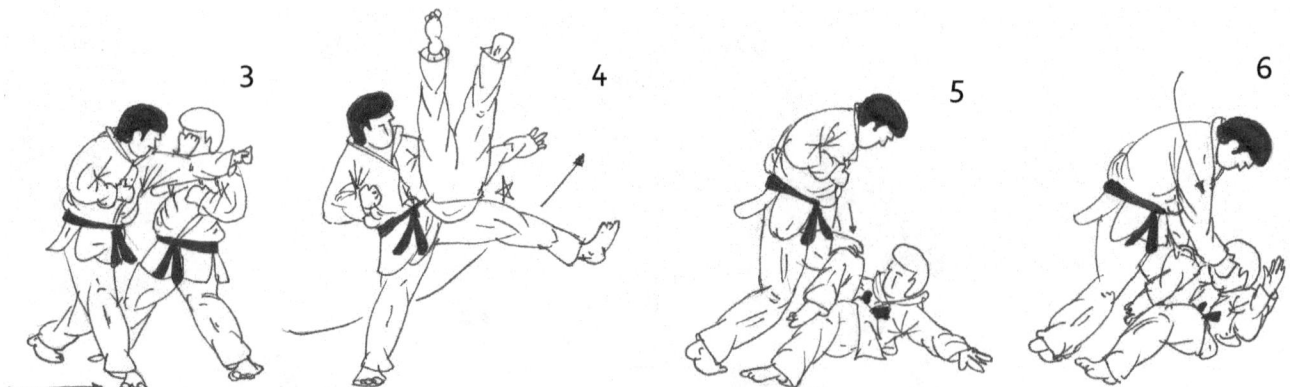

*The classic Hip Sweep Kick*

## Typical Application

As an application, the coming Figures will present *the Reverse Punch-entry variation*. The principle is the same. Your Reverse Punch entry is purposely long and in front of him. As soon as the sweep gets in, you can compound his fall by using the punching arm to push his upper body back and down. Control his legs as he crashes, in order not to be kicked if you follow to deliver a punch. Remember also that the technique works especially well against fleeing/retreating opponents.

*The Reverse Punch entry to the very surprising Hip Sweep Kick*

**Always be yourself, express yourself, have faith in yourself, do not go out and look for a successful personality and duplicate it.**
**~Bruce Lee**

# 27. THE GROUND PUSH KICK TO CHECKED HIP JOINT

## General

This is a technique of interest for MMA-type fighting, as you are lying down in front of a standing opponent. Should you be in such a position in real-life fighting, you should kick your opponent's groin; obviously not an option in a sport situation. In our present case, you will kick your opponent's hip while pulling his ankle, getting him down while hurting his hip joint.

## Description

The coming Illustrations show how you start at your opponent's feet. You immediately catch his heel or back ankle and *front-push-kick the hip of the same leg,* while pulling the grabbed foot forward. Simple and effective.

The basic
ground
Push kick to
Checked Hip
Joint

## Key Points

- This is a *kick* first, not a push.
- Kick *through the hip* with the mindset to damage it.
- Pulling the ankle forward is *simultaneous* to the Kick.

## Typical Application

The coming set of Figures shows how this is the perfect technique to use if your opponent gets up from being in between your guarding legs as you lie on the ground. As he starts standing up, get hold of his heel and punch towards his face with your other hand, in order to get him moving up and back more forcefully. Try to hook your opposite leg behind his other knee to keep him in check and help the coming Take-down. *Kick his hip while pulling the ankle of same leg* and while pulling the hooking foot behind his other knee (if you have it). Kick him as he falls down: a Groin Kick in self-defense or a Downward Heel Kick in sport. Keep at it.

*Use the Kick against an opponent standing up from inside your Ground Guard*

# Victory belongs to the most persevering.
# ~Napoleon Bonaparte

# 28. The High Stomp Kick to Arm-locked Elbow

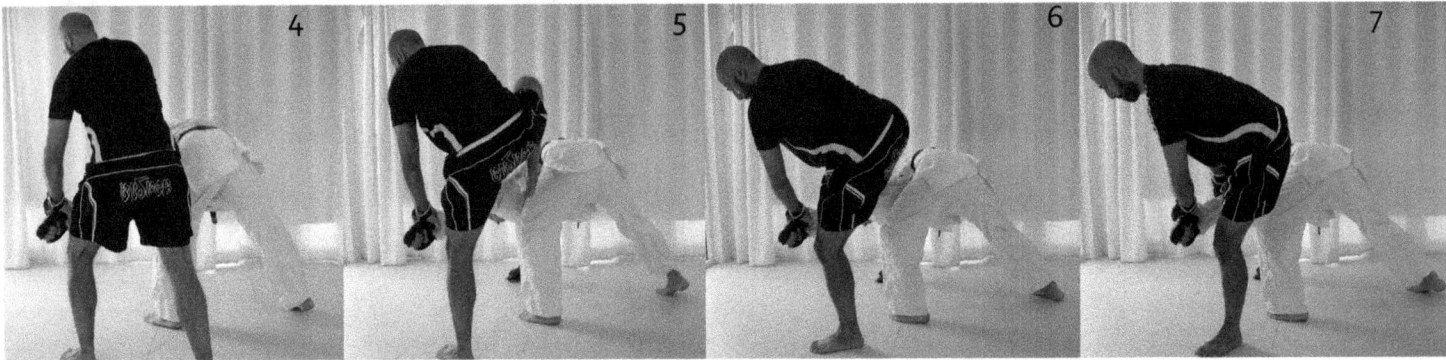

## General

This is a very specific but devastating maneuver. If fully delivered as a Kick, it will cause very serious and probably irreversible damage to the opponent's elbow and shoulder. Practice with extreme caution. It is pretty simple: you get your opponent in a classic standing Side Arm-lock, even briefly, and immediately lift your leg for a Stomp onto the elbow or the shoulder joint. It is pretty easy to execute, although it requires some flexibility.

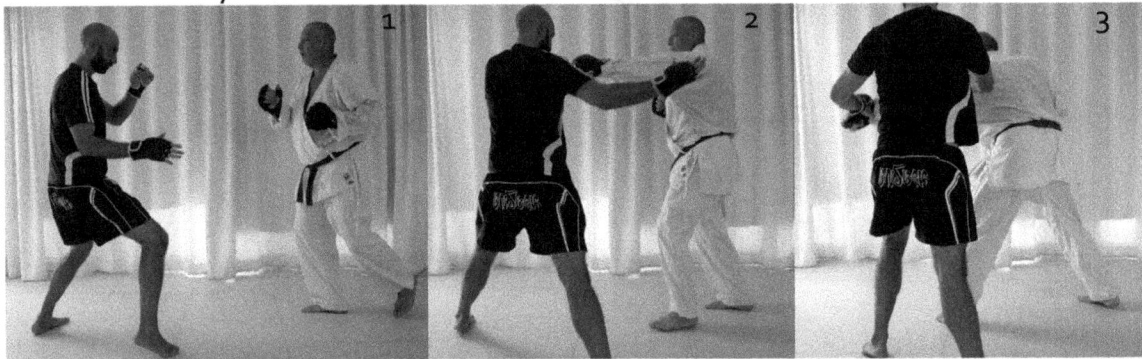

*The High Stomp Kick to Arm-locked Elbow*

## Description

In fact, this Kick can be delivered each time you have your opponent in a side armlock or even wristlock. It could be your automatic follow-up in case your opponent resists and fights the setting of lock!

The coming Drawings, at the top of next page, show how, from a very standard armlock position, you lift your leg high to stomp the locked arm somewhere between the shoulder and the elbow. In training, beware; in real life, *kick through and pull the wrist up.*

➡

*Pretty easy from a Side Armlock position*

*The Kick viewed
from another angle*

## Key Points

- *Kick*, do not push.
- Kick all the way *down to the ground.*
- Keep hold of the wrist as you kick. You can even *pull the wrist up.*

## Self-defense Applications

The coming Figures show the move as a follow-up of a typical **Wristlock**. A threatening assailant has an extended arm towards you. Do not wait for an attack, but grab his wrist in a classic Wristlock Hold. Twist the wrist and start setting the hold. An Inside-tilted Front Kick to the groin (or plexus) will bend him down for an easier Stomp Kick to damage the arm joints. Kick all the way to the ground.

*The Stomp Kick works as well on a good Wristlock*

The next set of Photos, at the top of next page, illustrates a **combined move**: a Crescent Kick to the head that also hits the arm, and then a rebounding of the leg into the Stomp Kick to the upper arm. The Crescent Kick mollifies the opponent and helps to set up the arm-lock low enough for the crushing Stomp.

➡

*Crescent Kick to the head followed by the Armlock and stomp kick*

This Kick should be used in any situation in which you can bend the opponent in classic armlock position. The example illustrated *at the top of next page* shows how **to evade and scissor-block a punching attack**. As soon as you can bend him down with the armlock leverage, stomp his shoulder, and then his elbow.

A way to mollify him in order to make sure he gets into the preferred position is presented *in a second set of Drawings,* on next page: pull his front hand violently and use a Roundhouse Chamber to attack his elbow joint from sideways and above. This will easily get him into Side Armlock position in which you can stomp his shoulder and/or elbow.

➤

*THE HIGH STOMP KICK TO ARM-LOCKED ELBOW*

*Always in classic side armlock position: stomp the shoulder and the elbow*

*Knee Strike down onto an extended elbow will get the opponent into Side Armlock position for a follow-up*

The following Drawings, *at the top of next page*, illustrate a very practical **Ground version** of the technique. In a grappling situation, or directly after a Takedown, you have caught your opponent in a classic and very automatic Judo Pin (The *Hon Kesa Gatame* Immobilization technique). It is a very good transitory control technique in which you use your body weight to keep him on his back while neutralizing his arms. Of course, in real fighting 'where everything goes', this can only be part of a dynamic maneuver. You will therefore immediately headbutt him in the face or on the side of the head to mollify him and divert his attention. Catch the wrist of his controlled arm while leaning on him, and lift your 'rear' leg to stomp his wrist down while his elbow is blocked on your front leg. This is a very damaging technique: be careful in practice. Keep his arm hyperextended with your legs, so as to free your hand to punch him in the face: he is totally at your mercy

**1**

**2**

*Ground Application of the Joint Kick in Hon Kesa Gatame Pin control*

**3**

**4**

**5**

# The purpose of training is to tighten up the slack, toughen the body, and polish the spirit.
## ~Morihei Ueshiba

*THE HIGH STOMP KICK TO ARM-LOCKED ELBOW*    **157**

# 29. Leg Hyperextension Techniques

## General

These techniques are *not* Joint Kicks per se, but important relatives. They are typical of East-Asian Arts and extremely damaging. They are based on causing the opponent to fall violently into a coerced 'splits' position. Even if you are flexible, the violence and the extent of stretching you will be subjected to will tear muscles and ligaments.
We shall only present applied examples to make things clear and easy.

## Self defense Applications

These techniques are based on blocking and grabbing the kicking leg of an attacker. The first example shows how to evade and rear-block an incoming Side Kick. The Block becomes a Scoop and you lift the leg brusquely on to your shoulder while attacking the attacker's face to mollify him. With his foot on your shoulder, you get closer by grabbing the back of his neck and punch him in the face with your (formerly) blocking hand. With his attention up, you will now violently kick his standing knee with a Low Front Kick. The purpose of the Kick is to hurt the joint and to push his foot back for what will follow! You pull your kicking foot very deeply back and go down on your knee. This is to be executed brusquely in order to pull his legs apart. Be careful in training!

*Grab a kicking leg and pull it apart from the standing leg to tear muscles*

It is clear to the trained reader, from the Illustrations of the previous example, that the technique can be applied on all kick types, and not only Side Kicks. This stays true for the next example as well. The Drawings illustrate how to evade back and absorb a Penetrating Side Kick, and how to grab the kicking foot by slapping it simultaneously from up and down. Pull the leg away and catch the foot by the toes with one hand and the heel with the other. Attack the extended knee of the grabbed leg with your own knee; this should hurt the opponent's joint (if you make sure you pull the leg simultaneously). You should then consider the Knee Strike as a chambering for the smoothly following Inside Front Kick to the opponent uncovered groin. *That* should mollify him! Now you will twist his foot violently to the inside while pulling your kicking leg way back behind you. Go down and back while landing on your knee. Concentrate on hyperextending his legs and groin area. This his very dangerous and painful, and it is even compounded by the Ankle Twist. Be extremely careful in training!

*Absorb a Side Kick, grab and knee the attacking knee before brutally hyperextending the leg*

# AFTERWORD

Here we are after this basic exploration of most Joint Kicks.

It should be now clear to the reader that Joint-kicking is more *a matter of the mind* than of physical techniques. Joint Kicks are basically regular kicks, but they are delivered towards the opponent's joints with the purpose of causing crippling damage. And that is a matter for the mind.

Many bouts of combat sports allowing low kicking do not end in busted knees. This is because the mindset is not about joint damage. The kicks will generally attrite the thigh to sap the will of the opponent and limit his will to move and attack.

Attacking the joints is a focused mindset that is important to acquire for real life situations. It comes within the 'Martial' part of Martial Arts.

It is not by accident that the most recurring kick in traditional Japanese *Shotokan Karate Katas* (formal exercises) is basically a foot Stomp. This very common '**Fumikomi**' kicking technique usually comes as a very wide and energetic Inside Crescent Kick that ends in low 'Horse' (*Kiba Dachi*) position on the opponent's foot.

*Fumikomi in traditional Katas*

*The Applied modern version of the traditional technique*

And this leads me to another point: a Joint Kick needs not be sophisticated. Simply stomping the toes of the opponent will cause him tremendous pain and will probably hamper his future ability to move. Stomping on the fingers of a downed opponent will be as crippling and take the specific limb out of commission to attack you. Of course, you need to stomp hard, but the general idea is clear. Simple and easy kicks directed to sensitive joints will do lots of damage, without the need for sophisticated jumps and turns. Most *Low Kicks* presented in previous work can be easily turned into redoubtable Joint Kicks.

Joint Kicks are important for the serious Martial Artist because they are the only way to fully ensure victory in a real-life conflict. Only by destroying the physical infrastructure that allows the opponent to keep fighting, can you fully stop him. Some people are relatively impervious to pain in stressful situations, and the human body can absorb lots of punishment before giving up. But if you damage the fingers, wrist or elbow of an assailant, he will not be able to use this limb to attack you further. If you damage his ankle, knee or hip, he will have difficulty to move effectively and to kick. If you stomp the knee or the ankle of a downed opponent, he will not be able to run after you; and if you stomp his Achille's tendon, he will be seriously crippled. On the other hand, people that have been kicked in the groin or punched in the face or plexus, can often keep fighting, sometimes enraged even more. [*This is where Krav Maga 'Retzev' principle comes in: once you have scored, you do not stop hitting until full victory*].

So, training for joint-kicking has to be done in two parallel ways: you have **first** to master the basic kicks and learn to impart maximum kick-through power. Use the heavy bag, the focus target and the old tire; but work at it for *power*.
**In parallel** you have to drill the targeting of the joint, carefully, with a partner, in set drills and in light free-fighting. Remember that it is your mind that you are training. Look for the joint attack in all possible situations and get familiar with the move.
If you seriously train this way, you'll be ready for a possible real encounter in which joints are a legitimate target.
And if, hopefully, you never have to get in such situation, you have been preserving Martial skills that are an integral part of the Arts.

It is all about training. Get to work!

**I fear not the man who has practiced 10,000 kicks once, but I fear the man who has practiced one kick 10,000 times.**
**~ Bruce Lee**

And now, dear reader, what is left is for you to start sweating.

**Pain is the best instructor, but no one wants to go to his class.**
**~Choi, Hong Hi, Founder of Taekwon-Do**

*<u>If you have enjoyed the book and appreciate the effort behind this series, you are invited to write a short and honest review on Amazon.com...It</u> has become extremely difficult to promote one's work in this day and age, and your support would be much appreciated. Thanks!*

All questions, comments, additional techniques, special or vintage Photos about Kicks and Krav Maga are welcomed by the author and would be introduced with credit in future editions. Just email:**martialartkicks@gmail.com**

The author is trying to build a complete series of work that, once finished, could become an encyclopedic base of the whole of the Martial Arts-Kicking realm, a base on which others could build and add their own experiences.

In his endeavors the author has already penned:

- **The Essential Book of Martial Arts Kicks** – *Tuttle Publishing* (2010)
- **Plyo-Flex** - Training for Explosive Martial Arts Kicks (2013)
- **Low Kicks** - Advanced Martial Arts Kicks for Attacking the Lower Gates (2013)
- **Stop Kicks** – Jamming, Obstructing, Stopping, Impaling, Cutting and Preemptive Kicks (2014)
- **Ground Kicks** – Advanced Martial Arts Kicks for groundfighting (2015)
- **Stealth Kicks** - The Forgotten Art of Ghost Kicking (2015)
- **Sacrifice Kicks** - Advanced Martial Arts Kicks for Realistic Airborne Attacks (2016)
- **Krav Maga Kicks** - Real-world Self defense Techniques from Today's most effective Fighting System (2017)

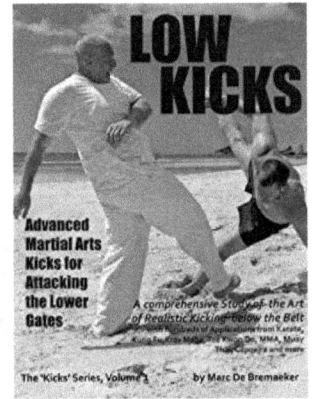

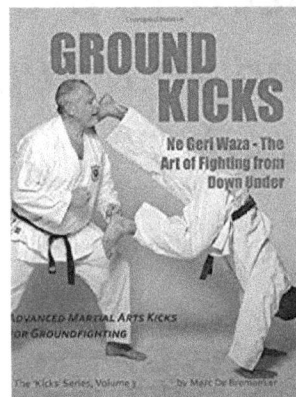

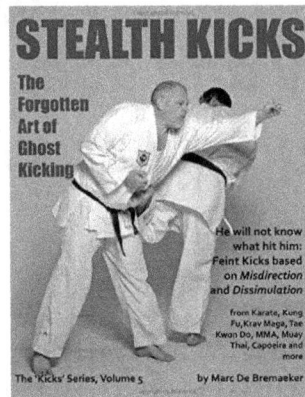

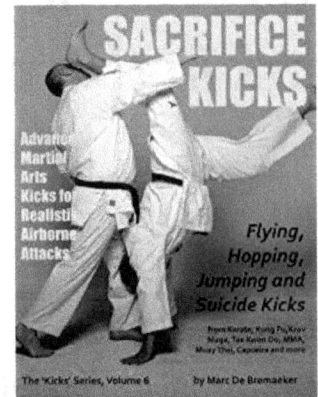

# Only one who devotes himself to a cause with his whole strength and soul can be a true master. For this reason mastery demands all of a person.
## ~Albert Einstein

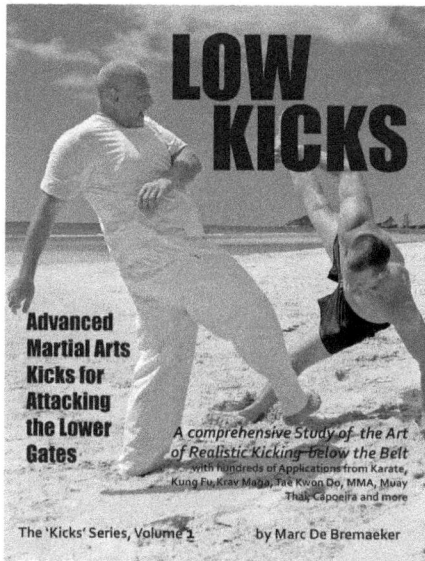

**Low Kicks** are powerful, fast, and effective exactly what you need to defend yourself in a real life confrontation. And because they are seldom used in sport fighting, they can be a surprising and valuable addition to your free fighting arsenal. While they may seem easy to execute, not all low kicks are simply low versions of the basic kicks. There are specific attributes and principles that make low kicks work. Marc de Bremaeker has collected the most effective low kicking techniques from Martial Arts like *Krav Maga, Karatedo, Capoeira, Wing-Chun Kung-Fu, MMA*, and *Muay Thai*. In this book, he analyzes each kick in depth, explaining the proper execution and outlining applications and variations from self-defense, sport fighting and traditional practice: Hundreds of examples in over one thousand photographs and drawings.

**Plyometrics and Flexibility Training for Explosive Martial Arts Kicks** and Performance Sports Plyo-Flex is a system of plyometric exercises and intensive flexibility training designed to increase your kicking power, speed, flexibility and skill level. Based on scientific principles, Plyo-Flex exercises will boost your muscles, joints and nervous system interfaces to the next performance level. After only a few weeks of training, you should see a marked improvement in the speed of your kicks and footwork, the power of your kicks, the height of your jumps, your stamina and your overall flexibility. Hundreds of illustrations and photographs will guide you through the basic plyometric and stretching exercises. Once you've mastered the basics, add the kicking-oriented variations to your workout for an extra challenge.

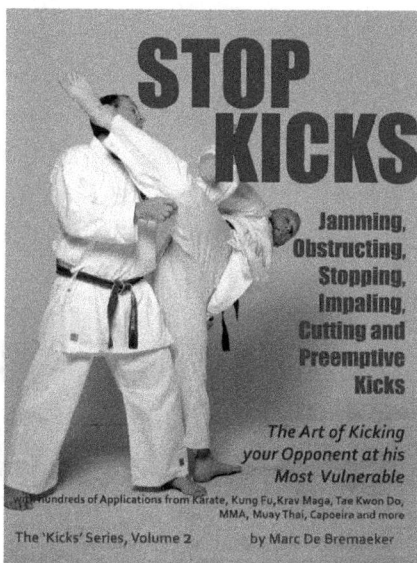

**Stop Kicks** are among the most effective, sophisticated kicks a fighter can use. And because they hit your opponent at his most vulnerable, they are also the safest way to pre-empt or counter an attack. Stop Kicks are delivered just as your opponent is fully committed to an attack, physically or mentally, meaning it is too late for him to change his mind. Hitting an opponent in mid-attack gives you the added advantage of using his attacking momentum against him. Stop Kicks: Jamming, Obstructing, Stopping, Impaling, Cutting and Preemptive Kicks presents a well organized array of stop-kicking techniques from a wide range of martial arts. Learn Pushing Kicks, Timing Kicks, Cutting Kicks, Obstruction Kicks, and Block Kicks from the hard-hitting styles of Muay Thai, Karatedo, Krav Maga, Tae Kwon Do, MMA and more.

Whether you are on the ground by choice or you have been taken down, whether your opponent is standing or is on the ground with you, whether you are a good grappler or you are trying to keep a good grappler at bay, whether you were caught unawares sitting on the floor or you have evaded down on purpose, whether you are a beginner or an experienced martial artist...this book has the right kick for the situation. In **Ground Kicks**: Advanced Martial Arts Kicks for Ground-fighting from Karate, Krav Maga, MMA, Capoeira, Kung Fu and more, Marc De Bremaeker has created a comprehensive collection of Ground Kicks, with hundreds of applications for sport fighting and self-defense situation. Packed with over 1200 photographs and illustrations, Ground Kicks also includes specific training tips for practicing each kick effectively.

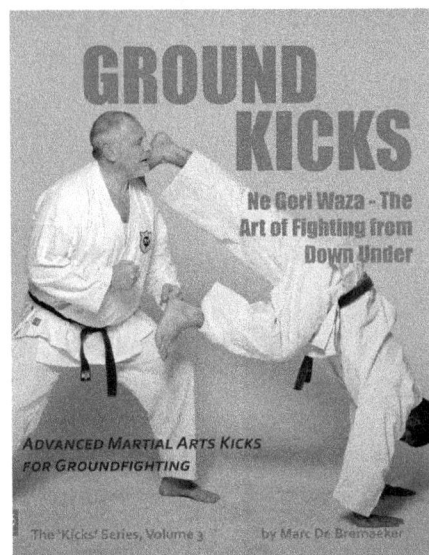

**Stealth Kicks** will introduce you to the Art of executing Kicks that your opponent will not see coming. This subject has never been treated comprehensively before. Whether you are a beginner or an experienced Artist, you will find suitable Kicks or tips to modify your current techniques to give them stealth. It will help you to score in Sport confrontations or make sure to come on top in real life Self-Defense situations. The *Feint Kicks* presented are based on misdirection: they will aim at provoking a misguided reaction that will open your adversary to the real kick intended. The *Ghost Kicks* presented are based on dissimulation and will travel out of your opponent's range of vision to catch him unawares. Together with general feinting techniques and specific training tips, hundreds of applications will introduce you to the sneaky Art of stealth kicking and will make you a better and unpredictable fighter. Crammed with over 2300 photos and drawings for an easy understanding of the concept of Stealth.

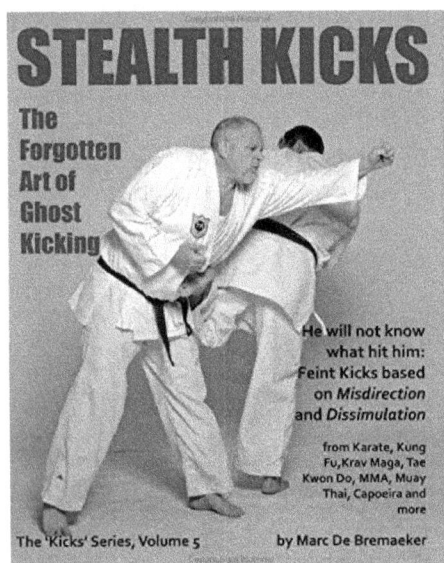

'**Sacrifice Kicks**' will comprehensively present the most important Martial Arts Airborne Kicks: Flying Kicks, Hopping Kicks, Jumping Kicks and Suicide Kicks. They have been dubbed 'Sacrifice' in the spirit of Judo's redoubtable Sutemi Takedowns in which one sacrifices his balance in order to throw his opponent down. *Flying Kicks* are not about showmanship, they are very effective techniques when used judiciously. They need not be necessarily high and spectacular; they can be surprising *Jumping Kicks* and *Hopping Kicks* executed long and low. And *Suicide Kicks* take the Sacrifice principles a little further: they are extremely unexpected techniques delivered airborne, but with little hope of landing on one's feet, unlike classic Flying Kicks. All these realistic maneuvers, coming from Karate, Krav Maga, Kung Fu, TaeKwonDo, MMA, Capoeira, Muay Thai and more, are described with applications and training tips. Over 1000 Photos and Illustrations.

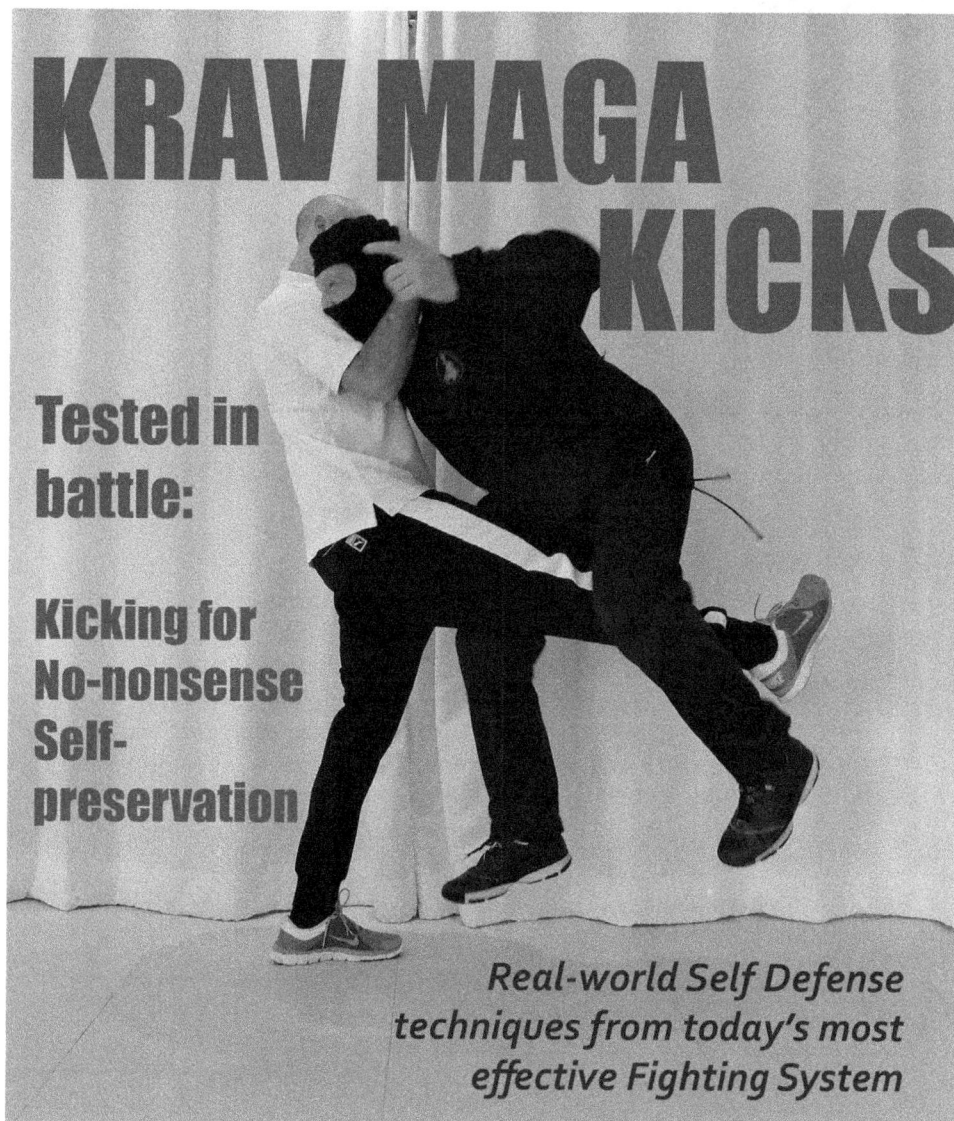

# KRAV MAGA KICKS

## Tested in battle:

## Kicking for No-nonsense Self-preservation

*Real-world Self Defense techniques from today's most effective Fighting System*

*Krav Maga* is recognized as one of the most efficient fighting systems around today. Based on common sense, it has evolved by necessity in a region ravaged by fighting for over a century. The first part of this book details and illustrates the preferred Kicks used in Krav Maga, and the second part presents the vital points to be targeted when kicking or striking. The Last part of this work is basically a full Krav Maga Self-defense course that also includes offensive techniques. The defenses against strikes, kicks, grabs, holds and chokes do often include kicking, but only when it is the most adequate reaction. This book is the first to underline in print the important principle of *Retzev*, with dozens of examples of continuous motion until the opponent is fully vanquished. Suitable for beginners and trained Martial artists from other Schools. **Over 1500 Photos and Illustrations!**

# OTHER GENRES FROM FONS SAPIENTIAE

AVAILABLE IN PAPERBACK AND KINDLE FORMATS ON AMAZON

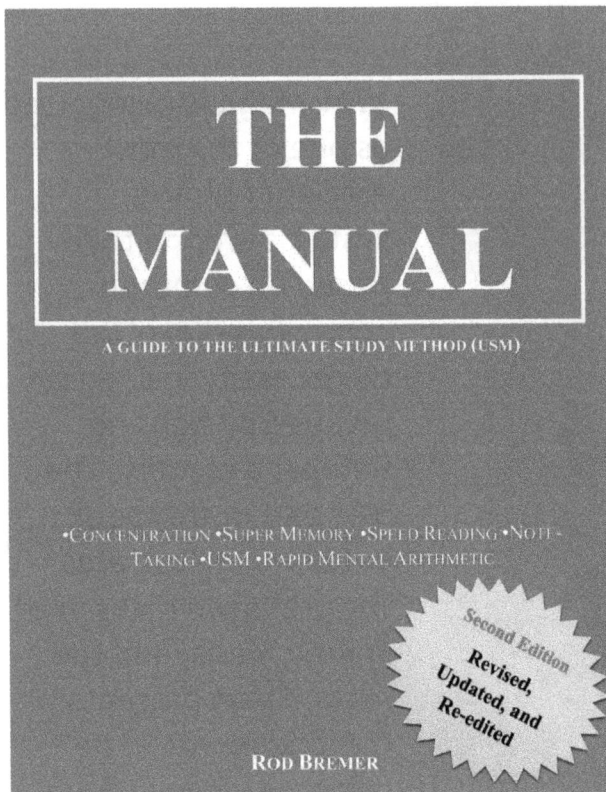

THE MANUAL

A GUIDE TO THE ULTIMATE STUDY METHOD (USM)

•CONCENTRATION •SUPER MEMORY •SPEED READING •NOTE-TAKING •USM •RAPID MENTAL ARITHMETIC

Second Edition
Revised, Updated, and Re-edited

ROD BREMER

**The Manual** is the definitive guide to Enhanced Concentration, Super Memory, Speed Reading, Note-Taking, Rapid Mental Arithmetic, and the *Ultimate Study Method* (USM).

The techniques presented are the culmination of decades of practical experience combined with the latest scientific research and time-tested practices. The system described herewith will allow the practitioner to:

• Read faster with higher comprehension.
• Remember any type of information instantly.
• Store information in long-term memory.
• Enhance concentration and focus.
• Access deeper levels of the mind.
• Induce relaxation.
• Rapidly perform complex mental arithmetic.
• Master the Ultimate Study Method (USM).

**USM** is a synergistic combination of established techniques for Concentration, Long-Term Memory, Speed Reading, and Note-Taking. It involves a systematic procedure that allows the practitioner to study any topic fast, efficiently and effectively. USM can be applied to all areas of educational study, academic research, business endeavours, as well as professional life in general.

**Rain Fund**: A riveting thriller

"...For the safety of the readers, this book ought to come with the disclaimer: leave this book read half-way at your own risk. Unless you are Superman, you won't be able to concentrate on much else until you have read the last page of "Rain Fund". The time has come for Patterson, Ludlum, Dan Brown et al to slide over and make space at the top for Marc Brem." - Shweta Shankar for Readers' Favorite

"...In the good tradition of Ludlum and Grisham. Five Stars" Aldo Levy

"Autistic geniuses charting financial markets; Mobster-fuelled Ponzi schemes; sophisticated hardware viruses; spies; and a rising superpower that strives for dominance – so realistic it is frightening."

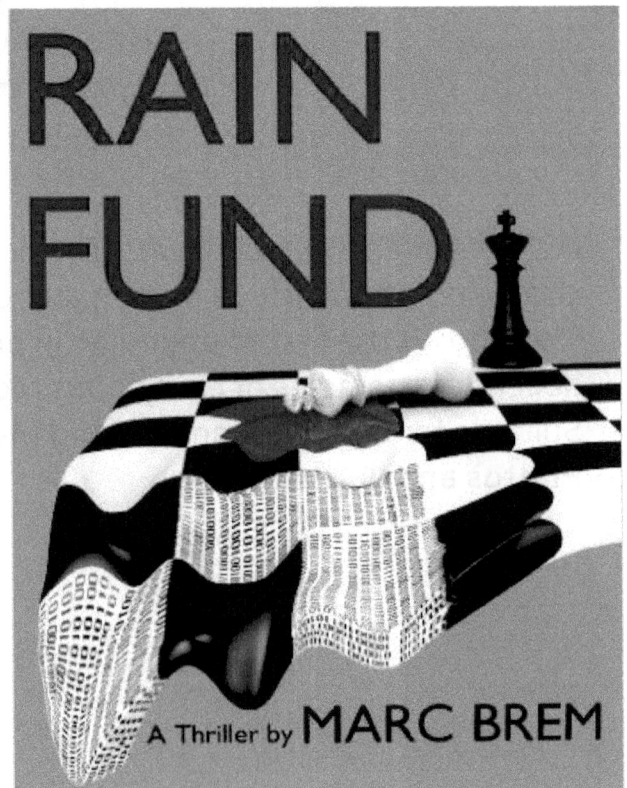

RAIN FUND

A Thriller by MARC BREM

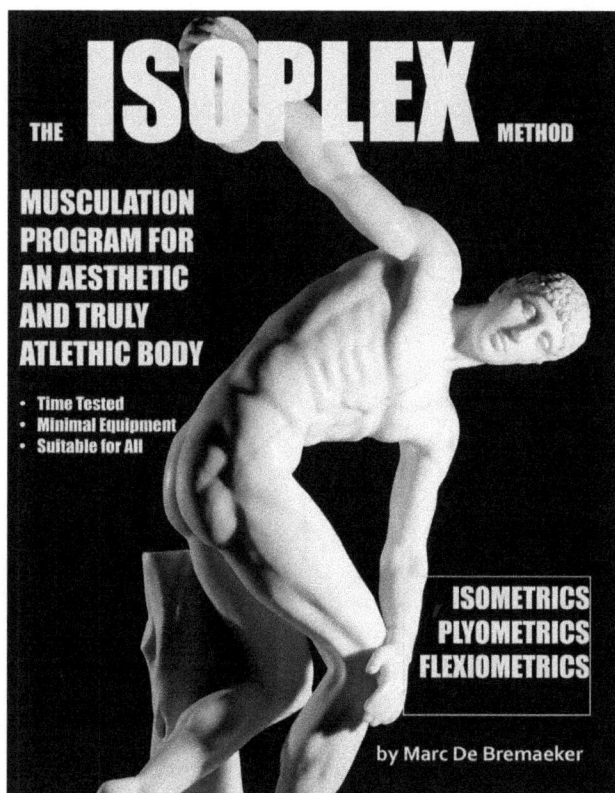

THE **ISOPLEX** METHOD

MUSCULATION
PROGRAM FOR
AN AESTHETIC
AND TRULY
ATLETHIC BODY

• Time Tested
• Minimal Equipment
• Suitable for All

ISOMETRICS
PLYOMETRICS
FLEXIOMETRICS

by Marc De Bremaeker

_Isoplex_ stands for Isometrics, Plyometrics and Flexiometrics. The well-organized combination of these three training methods will give the serious trainee the most effective path possible to powerful and aesthetic muscles, in a minimum of time. The method is simply the optimal combination of those three basic tenets of fitness training. It is suitable for men and women. It is suitable for beginners, for athletes of all types, and even for bodybuilders. It is designed to build an aesthetic physique which is also conducive to sport performance and to personal health. ISOPLEX is in fact the modern and more scientific version of the training ideals of Greco-Roman Antiquity. As illustrated by many well-known antique sculptures, the athletes of old had aesthetic bodies based on core musculature and long, well-defined and necessarily efficient muscles. These synergistic training principles are and were universal. They were to be found in ancient Asian Martial Arts and in Body Cultures like Yoga, Chi Kung and many others. A truly athletic and functional body needed for realistic fighting was achieved by a mixture of Isometric exercises, intensive flexibility training and dynamic (Plyometric) drills. Martial Artists and Yogis will immediately grasp the connection. This is the way to train the body for effective and natural aesthetics, and that is what Isoplex concentrates on through an optimal and synergistic time-saving program.

With hundreds of Photos and Drawings and detailing Five complete weekly Programs for all levels.

**JOINT KICKS**